Rewrite
Right!

Rewrite

Your Guide
to
Perfectly
Polished
Prose

Right!

Second Edition

Jan Venolia

Author of *Write Right!*, *Better Letters*, and *Kids Write Right!*

Ten Speed Press

BERKELEY • TORONTO

1🖚

Ten Speed Press
Box 7123
Berkeley, California 94707
www.tenspeed.com

Distributed in Australia by Simon & Schuster Australia, in Canada by Ten Speed
Press Canada, in New Zealand by Southern Publishers Group, in South Africa by
Real Books, in Southeast Asia by Berkeley Books, and in the United Kingdom and
Europe by Airlift Book Company.

Cover design by Paul Kepple
Book design by Tasha Hall
Copyediting by Suzanne Byerley
Illustrations by Ellen Sasaki
Excerpt from a Donella Meadows column on pp. 59–60 was first published in *The
Global Citizen*, December 18, 1999. Reprinted with permission.

Library of Congress Cataloging-in-Publication Data on file with the publisher.

Printed in Canada
First printing, this edition, 2000

1 2 3 4 5 6 7 8 9 10 — 05 04 03 02 01 00

> Mend your speech a little,
> lest it mar your fortune.—*Shakespeare*
>
> Mend your writing, too.
> —*Jan Venolia*

Contents

1 Why Rewrite?

> I have rewritten—often several times—
> every word I have ever published.
> My pencils outlast their erasers.
> —*Vladimir Nabokov*

As a writer or editor today, you have a lot more at your disposal than pencils and erasers.

- Word-processing software simplifies writing and revising, from note-taking and first drafts to final copy.

- The Internet is a reference library at your fingertips.

- E-mail makes keeping in touch with colleagues, friends, and family a snap and eases the interaction among authors, editors, peer reviewers, project managers, and production staff.

These powerful tools *help you do it,* but a solid foundation in the principles of revising tells you *what needs to be done*.

Rewrite Right! is for people who must write at work or in school and for freelance writers struggling to make sales. Editing is improving something written—making it easier to follow, snappier, more interesting. Knowing how to edit means

1

knowing what good writing is in the first place. And good writing comes from knowing how to revise, how to tug on words and adjust them until they say what you want them to say. In other words, writing and editing are facets of the same subject: doing a good job of putting ideas into words.

Have advances in telecommunications reduced the need for good writing? Not at all. The medium may change, but the language still needs to be well crafted. People who used to step down the hall to brainstorm with a colleague now sit down at a keyboard and whip out a message on e-mail.

E-mail has many advantages. It's convenient, fast, cheap, and less intrusive than a phone call; it provides a paper trail and is easily distributed to a large number of people. It allows an increasing number of people to work from their homes.

But the very ease of e-mail can be a hazard. Many people have developed an e-mail style that's breezy and informal; they pay less attention to spelling and grammar than they would in a standard letter. Should they care about good writing? You bet! E-mail recipients shouldn't have to puzzle their way through a message riddled with misspelled or omitted words and confusing references. Don't let the informality of e-mail fool you into thinking sloppiness is okay. Spontaneity is fine; sloppiness can be dangerous in any communication.

Muddled instructions create confusion. Costly research is repeated because results are buried in an obscure, two-pound report. Boring writing is tossed aside unread. Slipshod writing breeds distrust, prompting readers to wonder if language is the writer's only area of incompetence.

At the other end of the spectrum, good writing gets things done. Its crisp, clear style requires less of the reader's time. Good writing lowers administrative expenses, lightens workloads, and suggests the writer is competent in other areas as well.

Yet when it comes to writing, many capable people falter. They may be experts at marketing or high-energy physics, but ask them to write it up, and they rely on worn-out expressions and stilted prose.

As a consulting editor, I've learned where most people need help. My first two books, *Write Right!* and *Better Letters*, provide simple advice.

Rewrite Right! is for those who want more. It describes two levels of editing: (1) to improve style and content, and (2) to correct language.

Rewrite Right! includes a variety of reference materials: lists of accepted abbreviations, hackneyed expressions, common redundancies, and irregular plurals. It suggests ways to make a document look better and explores sophisticated tools available to today's writers and editors. A glossary provides definitions of unfamiliar terms.

I hope *Rewrite Right!* helps you learn not only to write and rewrite well, but to enjoy doing it.

2 Writing and Editing in the 21st Century

> Don't be afraid to seize whatever you have written and cut it to ribbons. It can always be restored to its original condition in the morning.—*E. B. White*
>
> Especially if you have the right software.
> —*Jan Venolia*

Today's sophisticated software puts a dazzling variety of tools at your fingertips. Use them in the early stages of writing to take notes, outline, and create rough drafts. Use them in the revising process to explore various formats, insert and delete text, and rearrange paragraphs or whole sections. Use them in the final stages to add graphics and captions, introduce desktop publishing touches (e.g., borders, shading, drop caps), and print final, camera-ready copies.

The Internet as Writing Resource

The Internet is a rich source of information about writing and revising. There you will find the principles of good writing, lists of common errors, interactive quizzes, online dictionaries, guidelines for gender-fair writing, and compilations of web-based writing centers.

But you need to exercise caution, because some of the information is inaccurate or outdated. For example, William Strunk's classic, *The Elements of Style,* is online in the original 1918 edition, not the modern version edited by E. B. White.

The very quantity of information is daunting. Arm yourself with a clear objective for your web searches, so you will be able to screen out extraneous material and reap the benefits of having the world at your fingertips.

Outlining

An outline helps break through the intimidating nature of a blank page; you feel that you've begun and can see a path to the end. An outline forces you to think about which are the more important topics, the ones to be emphasized and buttressed with supporting detail.

If you choose a standard outline format (topic, subtopic, sub-subtopic), your computer will simplify the process. You can:

- Add topics and subtopics

- Change a subtopic to a topic and rearrange topics as your outline evolves

- Insert a block of text

- Display or print an outline by topic level or in its entirety

If you prefer a free-form, handwritten outline, with circles and spokes or tree trunks with branches, your activity is more like brainstorming. That's all right! Dump your ideas on the page and then look for ways to tie them together.

But whether you use a computer, index cards, flip charts and marking pens, or lined yellow pads, an outline is a powerful tool. By boiling down the essence of your writing into just a few words, an outline helps you discover imbalances, discontinuities, or omissions. It tells you if you've delivered on the promise implied by your headings. It ferrets out irrelevant material. Take the time at the outset to develop an outline—it will pay big dividends.

Writing and Revising

Word processors have blurred the distinction between writing and editing. The once sharply defined steps of writing, analyzing, and revising are now integrated into a more smoothly flowing whole. You revise as you write, and write as you revise. You can be more daring and experimental knowing that you can easily make changes.

Early on, establish a suitable format for your document. Determine the margins and spacing and then either create your own format or choose a prepackaged style that matches your needs. Left justification of margins (in which the text is evenly lined up at the left margin) is the norm, but with the click of a mouse you can choose full justification (text evenly lined up at both left and right margins). You have a wide variety of type fonts and sizes to choose from, and individual words can be *italicized*, <u>underlined</u>, or set in **boldface.** Footnotes[1], subscripts (H_2O), and superscripts (10^{-27}) are easy to add.

You also have a variety of ways to modify text. You can delete individual words, lines, paragraphs—whole chunks of text. You can move them to a better spot, using Cut and Paste. Did you misspell a name? Correct it throughout the document with Find and Replace. Need to remove double spaces following periods? Find and Replace is your ally.

If you use certain paragraphs repeatedly, as in resumés, proposals, or promotional documents, you can store such boilerplate (for example, in AutoText) and drop it in where you need it.

When I can't decide between alternative wordings, I type the choices I'm considering in brackets. Later, as I edit the document, I delete the rejected alternative with a click.

Software tutorials cover the basics of writing fiction, nonfiction, and drama. Some programs use a question-and-answer format to help you plug holes in a plot or strengthen weak characters. Programs for screenwriters simplify the formatting of dialogue by eliminating repetitive typing of names.

Whether it's relatively unsophisticated or state-of-the-art, your word processor is much more than a fancy typewriter.

---

[1]See? It's a snap.

Checking Spelling and Grammar

A spell-checker is a valuable tool for catching misspelled or unintentionally doubled words. But be aware of its limitations.

Spell-checked documents may still include incorrect words. A spell-checker assumes a correctly spelled word is the right word. If you write *thier house*, the spell-checker will point out your error. But if you write *there house*, your mistake will go unnoticed.

I laughed out loud recently when I read of someone reaching "the first wrung of the ladder." Wrong rung! Most of us don't want to be laughed at, so careful proofing with the frequent use of a dictionary is still necessary. (See Chapter 8 for rules to help you become a better speller.)

A spell-checker also assumes any word it doesn't recognize is misspelled, so it flags many correct words, including names, acronyms, compound words, and hyphenated words. You can reduce this nuisance by adding frequently used proper names or acronyms to the spell-checker's vocabulary.

Grammar-checkers are even more limited. They sometimes incorrectly flag text, on the one hand, and overlook obvious errors on the other. Here are some of the "errors" a grammar-checker found in a draft of this book.

- It suggested that "paper and pencil are" should be changed to "paper and pencil is." Evidently its operating rules for agreement of subject and verb don't include compound subjects.

- It wanted me to change "most of whom write poorly" to "most of who write poorly." That's just plain wrong. (See p. 122 for help with *who* and *whom*—especially if you are a programmer who writes software programs for grammar-checkers!)

- It failed to catch the incorrect apostrophe in "writer's and editors agree...."

A grammar-checker won't find ambiguous words or incomplete sentences. It won't tell you which words to capitalize other than "I" and the first word of a sentence. It doesn't force you to think about your audience or the logic behind your presentation. It doesn't catch faulty references or misplaced modifiers.

Is a grammar-checker worth turning on? I find it useful in determining readability. A grammar-checker lists the number of sentences, number of words, average sentence length, and average word length. It counts the words in the shortest and longest sentences and identifies both. It can help you find overworked words by listing them according to the number of times they appear. Some programs will calculate the school-grade level needed to read a document.

Tracking Revisions

The ability to track revisions has removed one of the hazards of editing online. Previously, those golden words you thought you could improve upon—and then changed your mind—might have disappeared entirely. Today's word-processing software allows you to highlight and keep track of changes made in the text, even when more than one person is making the changes.

Here are a few features commonly available:

- New material is underlined and added to the text; deletions remain but are crossed out. This allows you to see exactly what has been added and deleted.

- Changes made by different individuals appear in different colors; the identity of the individual can be revealed by clicking on a revision.

- Changes can be highlighted on the screen only or on both the screen and the printed document. The original can be compared with edited versions, side by side on the screen. Changes can be accepted or rejected—repeatedly—if you later change your mind.

- Non-printing notes or comments (for on-screen viewing) can be inserted; a block of text can be highlighted for later revision.

Editing via E-Mail

E-mail is a great timesaver when you need to circulate drafts of documents among authors, editors, and project managers who aren't just down the hall from each other. What used to take days by mail and express delivery services can now be done in minutes.

To be sure, zapping text from one spot to another introduces new hazards. You must deal with the possibility of viruses and of PC-Mac file incompatibility. If you are alert to the need to find and remove garbage resulting from attachment errors (for example, an em-dash appears as the word "emdash" instead of the dash itself), you will have overcome the main problem in sending manuscripts via e-mail.

You also need to be sure that everyone in the process is operating under the same guidelines. This may mean writing your own instructions (everything from a one-page memo to a small booklet, depending on the complexity of the project). Everyone needs to know how to flag alterations, queries, and comments within a document, and how to control various versions (original, revised, and final). But once you've established

EDITING BY E-MAIL

1. Author submits text to Project Manager/Editor (PM/E) via e-mail. Anyone whose e-mail programs resist attachments can cut-and-paste the text into the body of the e-mail message.

2. PM/E checks for viruses, and if necessary, converts the files into the in-house word-processing software. PM/E also cleans up any formatting garbage that may have been introduced in the transmission; PM/E creates a project file and forwards copies of the draft to the editor.

3. Editor makes corrections in boldface; any queries are bracketed with an agreed-upon symbol such as a double plus sign, to avoid being confused with the text. The edited copy becomes the master copy, which is e-mailed back to the author using cut-and-paste to avoid introducing garbage (author is warned that no formatting will be seen in this version).

4. Author responds to queries and suggested changes right in the document, again using an agreed-upon symbol to set off any changes made. The resulting version is given a new file name to differentiate it from the original document.

5. PM/E puts both master copy and final draft submitted by author on screen, searches for the symbol, and then copies and pastes the alterations in the final draft into the master copy. PM/E sends master copy to production/layout and then on to proofreader.

6. PM/E sends paper copy to author for final check.

those procedures in your instructions, you'll find e-mail to be indispensable.

With such procedures in place, you have the desired, uniform results in a fraction of the time needed for sending hard copies around. In fact, you will probably wonder how you ever managed without e-mail.

Can you rely on software to do the whole editing job? No. In fact, the attractive appearance of pages created with state-of-the-art gadgetry may mask underlying flaws. The essential ingredients are still good judgment and your knowledge of writing fundamentals.

3 Getting Started

> No passion in the world is equal to the
> passion to alter someone else's draft.
> —H. G. Wells
>
> Unless it's the resistance to sitting down
> and editing your own.—Jan Venolia

The key to good rewriting is dividing the job into two parts: first-level editing, in which you tackle the substance of the writing (organization, content, style), and second-level editing, in which you correct the language (punctuation, grammar, mechanics). Second-level editing is also known as copyediting.

Two-Level Editing

When you wear both first- and second-level hats, wear only one hat at a time. Efficiency in editing comes not from a single, all-purpose reading, but from several readings, each with a different focus.

Look first at content and style. It's easier to detect abrupt transitions between paragraphs or poorly supported arguments in the first reading. Flag other problems for a later reading—and keep moving. You don't want to bog down in minor corrections when you're looking for flaws of organization and logic.

And you don't want to waste time punctuating a sentence that you later delete.

Look for specific types of problems in separate readings. Do verbs flip between past and present tense without reason? You can catch such disconcerting lapses more easily if you skim once looking only at verbs. Are the captions of illustrations and tables parallel in form? If you devote one reading to captions, you are more likely to notice inconsistencies.

Editing Someone Else's Writing

You face certain challenges when editing someone else's writing. It's easier to catch places where a reader might stumble; it's harder to deal with prickly egos. Making all the changes you think necessary while remaining on good terms with the author requires tact. Keep in mind that the author has already invested a lot of time, and your suggestions will probably call for an additional investment.

Avoid being confrontational: "That paragraph makes no sense," or "You're going to make us miss our deadline." Instead, look for ways to unruffle feathers: "I understand how you feel," "I'll take care of it," "Yes." Find ways to help the author convey ideas more forcefully.

Make sure what kind and amount of editing is desired. If you are expected to use only a light touch, look for errors in spelling and punctuation. Check for consistency of format, captions, treatment of acronyms, capitalization, compound words, and numbers. Such details contribute to smooth, orderly writing. You should also suggest substitutes for the author's pet words and reposition any misplaced modifiers.

On the other hand, if you are expected to review material for technical accuracy or readability, you haven't helped much if all you did was add commas or hyphenate compound words. Assume that something you find confusing or jarring will probably confuse or jar another reader, too. Be specific in letting the author know the nature of the problem by rewriting the troublesome parts.

Rein in overwritten prose, and point out areas where too much has been left out. Inject vigor where the writing is lifeless, and cool the rhetoric if the author is carried away with cleverness. But don't insinuate your personality into the writing, making it a crazy quilt of different styles. Above all, don't change an author's meaning. Handled skillfully, the author-editor synergy produces better writing than either individual could create alone.

Editing Your Own Writing

Being your own editor presents different challenges. It's hard to develop the distance needed for evaluating what you've

written. Take a break before
revising to help shift your
perceptions from writer
to reader. See the
document with
fresh eyes, as
if for the
first time.

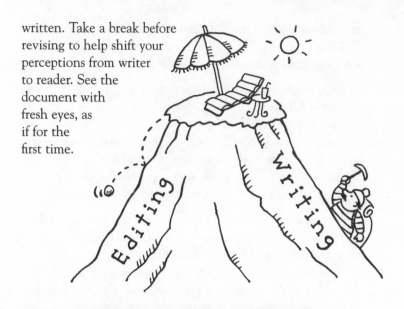

> Good writing is good manners. You can
> both please and help your public only
> when you learn how to be the first victim
> of your writing, how to anticipate a reader's
> difficulties, and to hear yourself as others
> hear you.—*Ritchie R. Ward*

An editing checklist is a good way to begin. It asks questions
to get you started and confirms that you haven't overlooked
anything important.

The checklist on pp. 19–22 serves a dual purpose: (1) It
reviews the fundamentals of writing and revising; (2) it
acquaints you with the contents of this book.

AN EDITING CHECKLIST

First-Level Editing: To Improve Writing
  Audience:
— Is the writing directed to a specific reader or type of reader?
— Does the writing match what is known about the audience?
— Does the approach take the reader's level of knowledge into account?
  • For a lay audience, are terms defined? Examples provided?
  • For an audience of experts, are enough supporting facts presented?
  • Are conclusions backed up by evidence?
— Do examples help the reader understand?
— Are answers provided for the questions readers are most likely to ask?
— Does the writing have the right tone, the right amount of formality or informality?
— Is the writing bias-free?
  • Have you used slanted words, inappropriate labels, or stereotypes?
  • Have you given parallel treatment in matters of sex, race, age, and ability?
    See *Write to Your Audience*, p. 29.

  Logic:
— Are the ideas clear?
— Was there a plan? Was it followed?
— Is the information coherent?
— Is it presented according to a logical scheme?
    See *Have a Plan*, p. 37.

Interest:

— Does the title enlighten and intrigue?
— Are headings helpful?
— Does the beginning make the reader want to read on?
— Are important points emphasized?
— Is there variety in kinds of sentences, in sentence lengths, in paragraph lengths?
— Does the ending provide a sense of completion?

See *Grab Their Attention*, p. 43.

Clarity:

— Are any words or sentences ambiguous?
— Are antecedents clear? (Will readers understand what words like *it* and *this* refer to?)
— Are words specific rather than vague?
— Do you signal what's coming by such words as *but* or *therefore*?
— Have unintentional double negatives slipped in?

See *Make It Clear*, p. 53.

Brevity, Conciseness:

— Are there too many words?
— Are there redundancies?

See *Trim the Lard*, p. 64.

Usage:

— Do the words convey the desired meaning?
— Are singular and plural words used correctly?

See *Know Your Words*, p. 69.

— Are there overworked expressions?

See *Cut Clichés and Hackneyed Expressions*, p. 73.

— Do you use the active voice wherever possible?

— Have you avoided lifeless verbs (*to be*, *exist*, *occur*)?
— Are words unnecessarily hedged with qualifiers (*almost*, *somewhat*, *very*, *little*)?

> See *Speak Out*, p. 76.

— Does gobbledygook create a verbal smokescreen?

> See *Jettison Jargon*, p. 80.

— Do the words create the right kind of picture?
— Are metaphors effective?

> See *Evoke Images*, p. 83.

— Are small words like *a*, *an*, and *the* used correctly?
— Are contractions used correctly (especially *it's* and *there's*)?

> See *Watch Small Words*, p. 85.

Second-Level Editing: To Correct Language

Punctuation:

— Do punctuation marks help readers grasp the meaning?
— Is there any surplus punctuation?

> See *Punctuation*, p. 89.

Grammar:

— Do subjects and verbs agree?
— Do pronouns and antecedents agree?

> See *Agreement*, p. 114.

— Are pronouns in their correct case (*who* or *whom*, *I*, *me*, or *myself*)?
— Do pronouns refer clearly to their antecedents?

> See *Pronouns*, p. 121.

— Did you remove dangling and misplaced modifiers?

> See *Adjectives and Adverbs*, p. 125.

— Are the tense and mood of verbs consistent?

> See *Verbs*, p. 128.

— Are related parts of sentences or headings parallel in form?
  See *Parallel Structure*, p. 132.
— Are sentences complete (i.e., no fragments)?
— Are there any run-ons?
  See *No-Fault Sentences*, p. 132.

Mechanics:
— Are abbreviations kept to a minimum? Are they used correctly?
  See *Abbreviations*, p. 135.
— Is capitalization correct and consistent?
  See *Capitalization*, p. 140.
— Are numbers below 10 spelled out? Are numbers of 10 and above written as figures?
  See *Numbers*, p. 149.
— Are words correctly spelled?
— Is the treatment of compounds consistent (as one word, two words, or hyphenated)?
  See *Spelling*, p. 152.
— If your writing includes quoted material, have the quotations been presented correctly?
  See *Quotations*, p. 161.
— Is hyphenation at the right margin minimized?
— Are words divided correctly?
  See *Word Division*, p. 162.
— Are there any gaps in page numbering?
— Are all tables and figures included and numbered correctly?
— Does the table of contents match the text?
  See *Document Integrity*, p. 165.
— Is the layout (format) attractive?
— Is it easy to read?
  See *Document Appearance*, p. 166.

Style Sheet

As you edit, use a style sheet to keep track of decisions you make about spelling (*esthetic* or *aesthetic*), capitalization (*Federal* or *federal*), and the treatment of compound words (*E-Mail, e-mail, email*). Style sheets are useful if you are the only editor, essential if two or more people are editing the same material.

To make a style sheet, divide a blank page into boxes. Put a few letters of the alphabet at the top of each box. Reserve a box or two for acronyms and numbers. When you come to a place in the manuscript where a style choice such as spelling or capitalization has been made, write in the appropriate box the term and page number where the word first appears. Thus, *subpoena* would go in the R, S, T, U, V box to show its spelling. *Low-grade infection* would go in the I, J, K, L, M box to show the hyphenation. Each time you encounter such a term, refer to the style sheet to see how you treated it before.

The principle is the same when you create a style sheet with your word processor. Instead of creating boxes, put the groups of letters flush with the left margin; as you come to an example in the text of a decision made, type the word or phrase under the appropriate letter.

Proofreading

Proofreading is the last step in the writer's quality-assurance program. It consists of comparing the "proof" (the printed pages produced by the typist or typesetter) with the author's final draft. The objective is to confirm that editing changes have actually been made and to catch any new typos or errors that previously escaped notice.

STYLE SHEET

A B C D

dialogue	53
bi-lingual	106
bodacious	12
Breathalyzer	46
ad hominem	73

E F G H

Federalism	72, 79
eminence grise	51
halftone	43
freelance	103-5, 110
European Common Market	79

I J K L M

middle-class junkies	66
machismo	67
lowercase	21, 23, 85

N O P Q

question-begging generalization	25
the Pentagon	89
Op-Ed page	66
palimony	67, 69

R S T U V

under way	153
renege	94
right-to-die movement	123
uppercase	21, 23, 86

W X Y Z

white-collar crime	15
win-win situation	12
X-rated films	34

NUMBERS

the 20's	12

ACRONYMS, ABBREVIATIONS

OPEC	34-7
IRA	59

Incomplete revision is an increasingly common cause of proof-reading error. A new wording is inserted, but remnants of the previous wording remain. For example, if you change "It can easily be distributed..." to "It is easily distributed..." but fail to remove one of the no-longer-needed words, the sentence will read, "It is easily be distributed...."

Authors should be the first to proofread their work. But since they often don't see their own mistakes, it's smart to have another person proofread as well. Important documents should be proofread by two people working together. One person reads aloud from the proof while the other follows along with the author's final draft. The reader should speak clearly and call out beginnings of paragraphs, italics, capitalization, and all punctuation marks.

If only one proofreader is a good speller, have that person be the one reading the proof. Presumably spell-checkers will have caught all the *misspelled* words by this stage, but there may well be *wrong* words (*site* instead of *cite,* for example). It's up to the proofreader to know if it's the right word.

If you don't have a proofreading partner, use two rulers to track the lines of text being compared. Keep the following questions in mind:

- Have any words or lines been left out?

- Have all deleted letters or words actually been removed?

- Have revisions created unacceptable breaks at the end of a line or page?

- Have any typos slipped in?

When you have made one correction in a sentence, re-read the entire sentence. In concentrating on the first error, you may have missed a later one.

> Typos that produce legitimate words are hard to catch and sometimes unintentionally funny. Here are some of my favorites—all of which would be missed by a spell-checker.
>
> Look for prescription drugs on which the patients have expired.
>
> The militia went into the countryside, fathering troops.
>
> The great steal of the State of New Jersey...
>
> The copulation statistics reveal a high level of mobility.

Make your corrections bold and clear. On double-spaced type-written pages, you can enter minor corrections between lines as long as the corrections are legible and understandable. On single-spaced or typeset material, place corrections in the margins, with a mark ($\wedge$) to indicate where to insert the change. If a change doesn't fit in the margin or between the lines, put it on a slip of paper and attach the paper, properly identified, to the page to be changed. Use sticky notes to remind yourself to verify a statistic or check a reference.

Run a "delete line" ($\mathcal{L}$) through letters, words, or phrases to be removed. Run a diagonal line through a capital letter you want to make lowercase.

If you change your mind about something you've crossed out, write "stet" in the margin. If you want to restore only part of the crossed-out material, put a dot under each letter you want retained.

If you add punctuation marks directly in the text instead of in the margin, mark them so they won't be overlooked. Circle any periods ⊙ or hyphens ⊖ ; put carets above commas ⌃ and below quotation marks ⌄ , apostrophes ⌄ , and footnote numbers ⌄ .

Proofreader's marks are an efficient shorthand; they originated in the printing industry but have been widely adopted. If you use these marks, be sure the person typing the corrected draft

PROOFREADER'S MARKS

ℯ	deleete	(tr)	transpoes
⌒	close up space		
#	insertspace	[	move left
ê/or	insert lettr punctuation word	]	move right
cap	uppercase	] center [	
l.c.	lowercase	(ital)	set in italic
stet	do not make correction	(bf)	set in boldface
¶	Begin paragraph.	(sp)	spell out
no ¶	no new paragraph		

understands their meaning. A photocopy of these marks
should do the trick.

(bf)] ^ MARKED-UP MANUSCRIPT [

¶ An American, instead of going in a leisure hour
to dance merrily at some place of public resort, as
the fellows of his calling continue to do
throughout the greater part of europe, shuts (cap)
home himself up at to drink.

no¶/(sp) He thus enjoys ② pleasures; he can go on thinking (tr)
of his business, and he can get drunk decently
drunk by his own fireside. . . . ¶In America I saw
the freest and most enlightened men, placed in the
happiest circumstances which the world affords.
[Yet] it seemed to me as if a cloud habitually hung
upon their brow, and I thought them serious and #
almost sad even in their pleasures . . . , forever
brooding over advantages they do not possess.
(sp)/l.c. --(A.) de Tocqueville, Democracy in America (ital)

Corrected Version:

A MARKED-UP MANUSCRIPT

An American, instead of going in a leisure hour to
dance merrily at some place of public resort, as
the fellows of his calling continue to do throughout the greater part of Europe, shuts himself up at
home to drink. He thus enjoys two pleasures; he
can go on thinking of his business, and he can get
decently drunk by his own fireside. . .

In America I saw the freest and most enlightened
men, placed in the happiest circumstances which
the world affords. [Yet] it seemed to me as if a
cloud habitually hung upon their brow, and I
thought them serious and most sad even in their
pleasures . . . , forever brooding over advantages
they do not possess.
--Alexis de Tocqueville, Democracy in America

4 First-Level Editing: Content

> No one can write decently who is
> distrustful of the reader's intelligence or
> whose attitude is patronizing.
> —E. B. White

Writing is only half of communicating; someone must also read and understand what you have written. Let's explore some ways to make your writing readable and understandable.

Write to Your Audience

Your audience may consist of many individuals, none of whom you know. Or you may be writing to a specific individual whom you know well. In either case, what you know about your readers' tastes, interests, and levels of sophistication should determine your approach to a subject and the tone of your writing.

Approach

Have you told readers what they need to know? When you're immersed in a subject, it's easy to lose sight of how much background the reader needs to grasp your ideas. Identify the readers you're addressing and aim for common ground. Start from a place that's familiar to everyone, then gradually introduce new information. In general, it's important to bring readers along one step at a time. If you give them too much information, too abruptly, they may abandon the effort.

When writing for a lay audience, define unfamiliar terms or concepts. Avoid such stiff and long-winded definitions as the following:

> Caisson disease is a disorder in divers and tunnel workers caused by returning too rapidly from high pressure to atmospheric pressure, characterized by pains in the joints, cramps, paralysis, and eventual death unless treated by gradual decompression.

Instead, you might define by the context:

> Divers who work underwater experience severe cramps and pains in their joints if they return to the surface too rapidly. This condition, known as caisson disease or "the bends," is prevented by increasing the time allowed for decompression.

or parenthetically:

> The divers return to the surface gradually in order to avoid "the bends" (severe cramping and pains in their joints).

Analogies and examples, especially ones with human interest, help make the subject matter accessible to a lay audience. Whatever your topic, explain the unknown in terms of the known.

> When a man sits with a pretty girl for an hour, it seems like a minute. But let him sit on a hot stove for a minute, and it's longer than an hour. That's relativity.—*Albert Einstein*

When writing for an audience of experts, your "launch point" is different. Only newly coined terms or those from another discipline require explanation. Expert audiences want the facts: what something costs, the size of the market, whether you can scale up from prototype to mass production. For a knowledgeable audience, you can economize on background information, but don't skimp on essential details.

If you know your audience is sympathetic, you don't have to sell your ideas. But an unconvinced or antagonistic audience requires different handling. Present your strongest arguments with no waffling. Imagine yourself as the reader; what counter-arguments or questions would you raise? Answer them. Does your answer raise other questions? Answer those, too.

Do you make recommendations? If so, present them early. Readers may become impatient following your thought processes step by step, not knowing your conclusions until the end. They want your recommendations up front ("what"), and then how you arrived at them ("why").

Slanted writing erodes your credibility. Avoid making empty claims (*fantastic results*), applying unfriendly labels (*big business, bureaucrat*), or using derogatory words (*fad, spurious*). Back up assertions, or readers will respond with "So what?" or "Why?"

Tone

When you're being interviewed for a job, you use one tone of voice. When you're having lunch with a friend, you use another. Similarly, tone in writing is formal or informal, high pressure or low key, partisan or objective.

A formal, businesslike tone is appropriate when reporting to a superior or applying for a job. The same tone would seem distant and cold when communicating with colleagues or seeking employees' suggestions. If you want to establish a friendly, informal relationship with readers, use plenty of first and second person (*I, you*). Make the tone conversational by using contractions (*you're, I've*). Don't be afraid to let your humanity show.

If your writing is more formal than you like, take a look at your vocabulary. Expressions like "It did not escape our attention..." instead of "We noticed..." sound pompous. Make your writing less stuffy with the following changes.

STUFFY:	BETTER:
accomplish	do
advise	tell
am in possession of	have
anticipate	expect
application	use (noun)
ascertain	find
by the name of	named
caused injuries to	injured
concerning	about
construct, fabricate	build
deem	think
desire	want
disclose	show
endeavor	try
ensuing	following
eschew	avoid
forward (verb)	send, mail
furnish	give
have need for	need
in lieu of	instead of
in the event that	if
indicate	show
initiate, commence	begin
is of the opinion	believes, thinks
kindly	please
lengthy	long
locate	find
methodology	methods
not too distant future	soon
partially	partly

STUFFY:	BETTER:
presently	now
prior to	before
procure	get
pursuant to	following, after, since
request	ask

A tone that is firm, honest, and reasoned fits most situations. Condescension ("As you should have been able to figure out by now...") and breezy intimacy ("We all know why that happened...") have no place in most writing. Irony and sarcasm backfire in the hands of all but the most skilled writers. Above all, be consistent by maintaining the desired tone.

> You can write about anything, and if you write well enough, even the reader with no intrinsic interest in the subject will become involved.—*Tracy Kidder*

Bias-free Writing. When the first edition of *Rewrite Right!* was published, bias-free writing was being hotly debated. Gradually the "person" jokes went stale and disappeared. Today most writers agree that it's just plain smart to remove bias from writing. The goal is to communicate, and that's hard to do if your words offend readers. The following guidelines will help remove bias from your writing.

- Do not mention race, gender, age, or disability unless it is pertinent. For example, look for the hidden assumptions behind marveling about an older person who runs or plays tennis. Is a sedentary life the norm for everyone over 60? I hope not!

- Avoid stereotypes and labels.

    Biased: The company picnic will be open to all employees, their wives, and families.

    Neutral: The company picnic will be open to all employees, their spouses, friends, and families.

- Use parallel treatment.

    Mr. Waxman and Ms. Stone, *not* Mr. Waxman and Linda

- Find substitutes for words that may be insensitive or confusing, such as the word *man* or masculine pronouns.

BIASED:	NEUTRAL:
anchorman	anchor
businessman	executive, manager, entrepreneur, merchant
chairman	chair
congressman	member of Congress
councilman	council member
draftsman	drafter
foreman	supervisor
layman	layperson, lay audience
layman's terms	non-technical language
mailman	letter carrier, postal clerk
man (noun)	human, humanity, human beings, persons, civilization, human race

BIASED:	NEUTRAL:
man (verb)	staff (e.g., *staff the booth*), operate, run, work
man-hours	hours, work-hours, staff-hours
manpower	personnel, staff, workers
repairman	service rep
salesman	salesperson, marketing rep
spokesman	representative, spokesperson
statesman	diplomat
workmen	workers

When you're referring to a specific male member of Congress or committee chair, it's acceptable to identify the individual as Congressman Ortega or Chairman Tyler. But if the term covers both women and men, or if it is open-ended, use a neutral term.

The committee will elect a new chair.
not The committee will elect a new chairman.

Here are ways to avoid using masculine pronouns.

Biased: Each applicant must submit his resume.
Neutral: Each applicant must submit a resume.

Biased: The consumer can stretch disposable income if he refrains from impulse buying.
Neutral: Consumers can stretch disposable income by refraining from impulse buying.

Awkward: Has someone lost his or her gloves?
Better: Has someone lost a pair of gloves?

Make your writing sensitive to both subject and reader. This doesn't mean removing all wit, flavor, and variety. You can remove offensive words and biased assumptions without resorting to clumsy solutions. As you become more aware of the subtle ways that bias creeps into writing, you will find easy and natural ways to make language bias-free.

Have a Plan

Put your ideas into writing before trying to organize them. If you're worrying about where they fit, you may lose some thoughts. Jot down the subjects in any order, regardless of importance: main points, minor points, examples, comparisons, background material. Write down whatever comes to mind about the topic. (See Outlining, p. 6.)

> Write freely and as rapidly as possible and throw the whole thing on paper. Never correct or rewrite until the whole thing is down.—*John Steinbeck*

When the "dump" of ideas from your head to the page or computer screen is complete, organize those thoughts into a logical scheme. In effect, you're creating a map that says to readers, "We're now at A; we're heading for B. Here's our route." Without such a plan, information is a jumbled heap of facts. By establishing a skeleton on which to hang details, you make the information accessible and more easily remembered.

Organizing

Organizing ideas is a two-step task: (1) group similar subjects, and (2) link the groups logically.

Grouping and Labeling. Readers find it difficult to grasp too many packets of information at one time. By combining similar items or ideas under a unifying concept, you give them a handle on the information.

Suppose you were asked to evaluate several office copiers. You could group your findings under labels that identify pertinent aspects:

- Major Features (speed, appearance, size)

- Additional Capabilities (document feeder, reduction, collation, stapling)

- Cost (initial, long-term, lease vs. buy)

- Maintenance (average time between service calls)

- Warranties (guarantee period, coverage)

Within these categories, you could label specific features as "Advantages" or "Disadvantages." You could also identify which capabilities are important for your office. Your approach depends on your purpose, but grouping and labeling make the information easier to absorb.

> The first rule of style is to have something to say. The second rule of style is to control yourself when, by chance, you have two things to say; say first one, then the other, not both at the same time.—*George Polya*

Linking the Groups. Next, link the groups of ideas in a logical scheme. The framework that best suits your purpose will take into account your readers' needs and interests and how ideas naturally come together. Here are five approaches to imposing order on writing.

STEPS IN A PROCESS: Describe procedures, step by step, like a recipe. *Use in instructions, operator's manuals, how-to articles.*

CHRONOLOGICAL: Trace the sequence of events: what happened and when. *Use in progress reports, biographical or historical sketches, accident reports, legal depositions, trip reports.*

ANALYTICAL: Present data, draw conclusions. *Use in annual reports, feasibility studies, investment memos, market surveys, consumer reports.*

COMPARISON: Emphasize similarities and differences or advantages and disadvantages. *Use in feasibility studies, surveys of competition, product comparisons, building site evaluations.*

GEOGRAPHICAL: Describe subjects by region. *Use in market surveys, sales reports, travel articles.*

Within such loose frameworks, you have still more choices about how to organize your information. For example:

- Most to least important (or vice versa)

- Least to most controversial

- Negative to positive (or vice versa)

- Deductive reasoning (from general to specific) or inductive reasoning (from particular to general)

When you are making a recommendation, it often pays to begin with your most important point. However, "least to most controversial" may be necessary if your readers need to be persuaded. "Negative to positive" will avoid your being charged with dodging issues; it also leaves readers on a positive note.

Typically, several methods of organization are used within one document, possibly within a single paragraph. An annual report, for example, could announce record earnings (*most to least important*), introduce new products (*analytical*), describe regional operations (*geographical*), report on the competition (*comparison*), and recommend how shareholders vote (*least to most controversial*).

Make each paragraph a coherent unit with a limited and well-defined purpose. One thought: one paragraph. Use the first sentence (the topic sentence) to tell what the paragraph is about (the thesis); relate subsequent sentences to the thesis. For example:

> Men make history and not the other way round. [Topic Sentence] In periods where there is no leadership, society

stands still. Progress occurs when courageous, skillful leaders seize the opportunity to change things for the better.
—*Harry S. Truman*

As you edit for logical organization, you may find an idea out of place or a major point buried in the middle of a paragraph. Rearrange the sentences until the pieces fit together smoothly.

Format

Format is important in identifying main topics and supporting ideas or information. Use spacing, numerals, headings, and underlining, italics, or boldface to emphasize key ideas. By efficiently identifying the main points, you give busy readers the basic thrust of your presentation.

Grab Their Attention

The attention of your audience may be assured if you are writing about a topic of interest to them—or if it's required reading. But even with a captive audience, clear, vigorous writing is a courtesy well worth observing.

Titles

The title is your first chance to catch the reader's attention. Is it informative? There should be no question what the subject is, yet the title needn't be dull or wordy. "An Overview of the Structural and Conceptual Characteristics of Future Planning Systems" strikes out on both counts. "Planning: System or Chaos?" might get you to first base.

A short title is easier to remember, so boil it down to as few words as possible, and then play with them a little. Does it help to phrase the title as a question? Perhaps the main title can be the attention grabber and the subtitle can flesh out the subject. Sometimes a play on words is effective, but being too cute is a hazard. Notice titles that you come across in your reading. What makes them work?

Headings

Headings are your next chance to catch the reader's eye. They provide information as well as visual breaks; they reveal the structure of your text, making it easier to locate information or follow the flow of ideas. A busy reader can skim headings to find the sections of most interest.

Headings can be single words:

Introduction	Conclusions
Analysis	Summary

phrases:

> Tracking Regional Performance
> Absenteeism under the Flexitime Program

complete sentences:

> Regional performance is uneven.
> Flexitime reduces absenteeism.

or questions:

> Are regional sales uniform?
> Will Flexitime improve productivity?

Make the style of comparable headings parallel. Use similar verb forms, noun phrases, or complete sentences to help a reader understand the relationship between different sections. Compare the following groups of headings. The first is a hodgepodge of verbs, nouns, and sentences; it's hard to see any relation between them. The second has parallel forms of action verbs that clearly present the topic (ways to use a video recorder).

AWKWARD:	PARALLEL:
Training Technicians	Train Technicians
Use Your Recorder to Screen New Employees	Screen New Employees
Time-and-Motion Studies	Document Time-and-Motion Studies
How to Improve Quality Control	Improve Quality Control

(See p. 132 for more about parallelism.)

Headings can be centered, flush left, indented, italicized, or boldface; they can be all capital letters or uppercase and lowercase. The text that follows a heading either starts a new line or is run in on the same line as the heading. Make the format of your headings consistent. The following examples are themselves illustrations of two different formats.

Here is one example of a heading format:

FIRST ORDER HEADINGS (all caps, centered)

Second Order Headings (italics)
Text follows on next line.
Third Order Headings (boldface): Text run in on same line.

Here is another heading format example:

FIRST ORDER HEADINGS (all caps, flush left)

Second Order Headings (boldface): Text run in on same line.

    Third Order Headings (italics): Indented, text run in on same line.

Openings

> Writing a first paragraph is like raising a
> first child. It's better if you start out on
> the second.—*Lynn Z. Bloom*

Writers often meander before getting down to business. If you're one of them, you may find that what you've written in the second or third paragraph is your strongest opening.

The goal is to get to the point quickly. Readers want to know what you are writing about and why it matters. This doesn't mean beginning with a plodding "The purpose of this memo (report, article) is to…." An effective beginning incorporates purpose indirectly, perhaps even dramatically.

> Isolation is one of the biggest challenges facing employees who work at home. Networking may give them instant communication with colleagues in Singapore and Riyadh, yet fail to provide the energy of direct human interaction.

Readers know what to expect from such an opening. It states the problem and suggests the scope of what follows.

Jumping right in with a recommendation is another approach.

> A mandatory day in the office every week offsets the isolation of working alone at home. Employees enjoy flexible hours and an easy commute, while management retains more direct control.

Emphasis

Are details supplied in proportion to importance? Is your main thesis diluted by lesser points? When you know more about a minor point than a major one, you may be tempted to display your knowledge with lots of words. Resist the temptation.

The way you construct sentences also subordinates one idea to another. Notice the change in emphasis in the following sentences.

> The new assembly line has produced some lemons, but genuine progress has been made.

> Genuine progress has been made, although the new assembly line has produced some lemons.

You can emphasize important points in other ways, too.

- BULLETS: Make short items stand out

- UNDERLINING OR ITALICS: Focus on topic sentences or stress specific words or phrases

- CAPITAL LETTERS: Provide a visual break or identify a brand name

- INDENTATIONS: Set off quotations or bulleted information

- NUMBERING: Identify groupings

An occasional question-and-answer format draws the reader into your line of thought.

> Is Flexitime the only way to reduce absenteeism? Obviously not.

A colon focuses attention on what follows.

> Leasing equipment has one major advantage: flexibility.

The order in which you present items also creates emphasis. Notice how the following sentences have a built-in kicker at the end.

> There are several good protections against temptation, but the surest is cowardice.—*Mark Twain*

> If you would know the value of money, go and try to borrow some.—*Poor Richard*

> Injustice is relatively easy to bear; what stings is justice. —*H. L. Mencken*

Variety
A series of declarative sentences (subject-verb, subject-verb) soon puts readers to sleep.

> Company profits fell 14% during the last quarter. Analysts attributed the decrease to foreign competition. Recovery is anticipated in the coming reporting period.... (snore)

You can break away from such monotony by varying sentence structure, sentence length, and paragraph length.

Vary Sentence Structure. Sentences are classified as simple, compound, and complex. A *simple sentence* is a subject and predicate (in other words, an independent clause—one that can stand by itself).

> <u>The polls</u> <u>closed at 8 p.m.</u>
> subject   predicate

A *compound sentence* is two or more independent clauses.

The polls closed at 8 p.m., and
independent clause

the ballots were counted within an hour.
independent clause

A *complex sentence* is an independent clause plus one or more dependent clauses (a dependent clause cannot stand by itself as a separate sentence).

Although the polls closed at 8 p.m.,
dependent clause

we had counted the ballots by 9:00.
independent clause

As you can see, each type of sentence has a different "personality." Simple sentences are a good device for making short or emphatic statements. Compound sentences work well with two closely related elements or ideas. Complex sentences are good for presenting background information or for subordinating one idea to another.

The following examples show how some eminent people have used all three types. Notice the variety of ways these sentences begin; different beginnings also make writing more interesting.

Simple Sentences:

There's no reason to be the richest man in the cemetery. You can't do any business from there.—*Colonel Sanders*

Having two bathrooms ruined the capacity to cooperate. —*Margaret Mead*

> Nothing so needs reforming as other people's habits.
> —*Mark Twain*

> A clear conscience is usually the sign of a bad memory.
> —*Anonymous*

Compound Sentences:

> I don't know the key to success, but the key to failure is trying to please everybody.—*Bill Cosby*

> I tape, therefore I am.—*Studs Terkel*

> The cost of living is going up, and the chance of living is going down.—*Flip Wilson*

Complex Sentences:

> Fanaticism consists in redoubling your effort when you have forgotten your aim.—*George Santayana*

> A government is the only known vessel that leaks from the top.—*James Reston*

> Read over your compositions and, when you meet a passage which you think is particularly fine, strike it out.
> —*Samuel Johnson*

Vary Sentence Length. Short sentences are effective for introducing a new subject, long ones for developing a point. Modern writing tends to favor sentences of roughly 20 words. But if a sentence is well crafted and not overloaded with ideas, you can stretch those boundaries with an occasional long sentence. Use word-processing programs that analyze sentence and word length to determine readability.

Vary Paragraph Length. How long are your paragraphs? Generous amounts of white space hold the readers' interest and avoid visual monotony. They also avoid intimidating readers with solid blocks of type.

Busy people often rely on a quick look at the opening of a paragraph to determine if they want to read the rest. It follows that more of the document will be read if it consists of short paragraphs. However, lots of one- or two-sentence paragraphs become monotonous and tend to de-emphasize everything on the page. Reserve the shortest paragraphs (even as short as one sentence) for the points you want to stand out.

Closings

> ...go on till you come to the end; then stop.
> —*Lewis Carroll*

How do you know when you're at the end? If you have clearly understood your objective in writing, you probably also know when you've achieved that purpose. You will have presented the information in digestible chunks, included supporting arguments, or provided explanations and examples. In short, because you knew where you were going, you will know when you've arrived.

What remains is to button it up. Are the conclusions you want readers to draw from your evidence clear? Present one last compelling argument to reinforce the main points. In long documents, summarize important ideas in a different way, rather than repeating yourself. Where appropriate, indicate the next steps to be taken. Make the ending provide a sense of completeness.

Stephen Jay Gould closed an essay on the search for intelligent life in outer space with a question.

> Ultimately, however, I must justify the attempt at such a long shot simply by stating that a positive result would be the most cataclysmic event in our entire intellectual history. Curiosity impels, and makes us human. Might it impel others as well?

In "The Gift of Wilderness," Wallace Stegner hammers home his message in a long and powerful last sentence.

> Instead of easing air-pollution controls in order to postpone the education of the automobile industry; instead of opening our forests to greatly increased timber cutting; instead of running our national parks to please and profit the concessionaires; instead of violating our wilderness areas by allowing oil and mineral exploration with rigs and roads and seismic detonations, we might bear in mind what those precious places are: playgrounds, schoolrooms, laboratories, yes, but above all shrines, in which we can learn to know both the natural world and ourselves, and be at least half reconciled to what we see.

Make It Clear

> Trouble in writing clearly...reflects troubled thinking, usually an incomplete grasp of the facts or their meaning.—*Barbara Tuchman*

Clear thinking is a prerequisite for clear writing. But even if your thoughts are muddled when you start, the act of writing often clarifies thinking. Your real purpose may become obvious only after you have struggled to write about it.

Writing is clear when readers get the point quickly and can follow supporting arguments. Any ambiguity or vagueness that gets in the way is bad writing.

Avoid Ambiguity
Have you left a reader in doubt as to the meaning of critical words?

Ambiguous: Child killers can be rehabilitated.

"Child killers" could mean people who kill children or killers who are themselves children. Your meaning may be so clear to you that you fail to see the possibility of other interpretations.

Ambiguous: She is helping the prisoners get off drugs and recording books for the blind.

This sentence suggests that the prisoners need to kick their habit of recording books for the blind, as well as their drug habit. Rewrite to avoid such booby traps.

Have you omitted any necessary words? Readers might wonder about the meaning of the following sentences:

Phil loves power more than his wife.

San Diego is farther from Los Angeles than Santa Barbara.

Less confusing versions would be:

Phil loves power more than he loves his wife.
or Phil loves power more than his wife does.

San Diego is farther from Los Angeles than Santa Barbara is.

Have you omitted necessary punctuation? The following sentences should have commas to prevent misreading.

After eating the negotiators returned to the bargaining session.

When the headlights are on an indicator light in the push button illuminates the switch.

As children grow the specific emotional lessons they are ready for include...

Even though I was young when she told me that I understood her meaning completely.

An omitted hyphen in a heading can also be misleading. There's a big difference between "Attack Dog Training" and "Attack-Dog Training." (See pp. 102 for more discussion of hyphens.)

Does the position of a word or phrase create ambiguity? In the following example, the employees might be in for an unpleasant situation.

> **Ambiguous:** I have discussed how to fill the empty containers with my employees.

> **Clear:** I have discussed with my employees how to fill the empty containers.

Revise Unclear References

Are your references confusing? When you write *it* or *they* or *her*, do readers know what those pronouns refer to? In other words, are the antecedents of the pronouns clear?

> **Ambiguous:** John Doe is the son of a plumbing supply salesman who died when he was 10.

Who was 10, the salesman or his son? We can make a good guess, but we shouldn't have to. Logic tells us that we must leapfrog back to the word *son* to find the correct antecedent for the pronoun *he*. Avoid putting readers through such gyrations (and giving them a belly laugh at your expense) by making sure each pronoun refers clearly and correctly to its antecedent.

The best solution may be to avoid using a pronoun.

> **Clear:** John Doe, the son of a plumbing supply salesman who died when John was 10...

Here are some other examples of unclear references and ways to correct them.

This, that, these, those. Are these words followed by a noun? If not, they are probably faulty references.

> **Unclear:** The staff has begun analyzing the chain of events that produced the increase in sales. This was long overdue.

This could refer to the analysis or to the increase in sales.

Clear: The staff has begun analyzing the chain of events that produced the increase in sales. This long overdue analysis will shape our marketing strategy.

Who. Does *who* refer to the preceding noun? In the following example, the preceding noun is *board.*

Unclear: The chairman of the board, who will be available for comment...

Will the board or the chairman be available?

Clear: The board chairman, who will be available...

It. Is the word that *it* refers to actually in the sentence?

Unclear: On the second day, the patient's knee was better, and on the third day, it had completely disappeared.

The word *it* obviously refers to a physical problem that isn't stated.

Clear: On the second day, the patient's knee was better, and on the third day, the pain had disappeared completely.

Which. Does an intervening phrase make the reader uncertain of the meaning?

Unclear: The report of the commission, which attracted so much media attention...

Does *which* refer to the commission or the report?

Clear: The commission's report, which attracted...

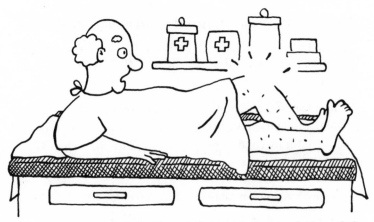

...on the third day, it had completely disappeared. (See p. 56.)

Frequently, removing prepositional phrases such as "of the commission" removes uncertainty.

Be Specific

Vague words fail to convey information. A general statement like "Product X saves you money" is unconvincing. It leaves unanswered the question "How?" Readers want the specifics: miles per gallon, infrequency of repair, warranties. Writing "She is a good employee" suggests general satisfaction with performance but provides no way to confirm that opinion. The more vivid and precise your words, the better the readers will understand and remember them.

> **Specific:** She learns quickly and is eager to increase her skills. When we acquired a Zaplex, she was the first to master the system. Her help in training the rest of the staff proved invaluable.

Being precise does not require that you be long-winded. One exact word often replaces several inexact ones. Furthermore, you can be precise with the plain words that many people use every day.

VAGUE:	SPECIFIC:
a better position	a 23% increase in profits
sanitary conditions	safe drinking water
extenuating circumstances	a broken leg
the present writer	I
a plumbing malfunction	a leaky faucet

Examples are a good way to make your writing specific. If you're reporting on the pros and cons of Flexitime, don't stop at citing "improved employee morale" as one of the benefits.

> Employees say they like having time off during the day. They use it for everything from teacher conferences to Christmas shopping. Medical appointments, physical-fitness programs, and special events such as a concert or ball game are easier to fit into their lives. Many add that they appreciate just being able to break up the daily routine.

Abstract words can highlight underlying concepts (e.g., productivity, labor relations). But unless you tie down the abstractions with particulars (number of units produced, freedom from strikes), readers have to guess at your meaning.

Syndicated columnist Donella Meadows illustrates the importance of vivid language. As she explores the idea that dry writing may be the reason why environmentalists have failed to convey the urgency of the global situation, she presents three versions of the same viewpoint.

> **First Version:** "Our massive tampering with the world's interdependent web of life—coupled with the environmental damage inflicted by deforestation, species loss, and climate change—could trigger widespread adverse effects, including unpredictable collapses of critical biological systems and interactions and dynamics we only imperfectly understand. Uncertainty over the extent of these effects cannot excuse complacency or delay in facing the threats."

Second Version: "People are devastating the environment. We are destroying forests, driving species to extinction, and changing the climate. Whole plant and animal systems may die before we understand how they function. Since we don't understand what we are doing, it is inexcusable for us to dismiss or ignore signs of danger."

Third Version: "We are wrecking nature without understanding how it works or how it supports us."

Meadows has a point.

Use Transitional Words

Certain words tell the reader what to expect. *But* or *however* warns that you're changing direction; *therefore* spotlights a conclusion. Without such transitions, the bridge between sentences is missing, and readers have no time to grasp the full meaning of one idea before the next one hits them.

Confusing: Not all patients do well; some fail completely. The overall results are good.

Clear: Not all patients do well; some fail completely. However, the overall results are good.

Jacques Barzun describes transitional words as the guiding touch to the elbow of someone you are piloting through new sights. Use the "guiding touch" of transitional words to pilot your readers.

TRANSITIONAL WORDS

To indicate a conclusion:	*thus, accordingly, therefore, so, hence, as a result, consequently*
To introduce examples:	*for instance, namely, for example, to illustrate*
To build a case:	*also, similarly, in addition, as well as, furthermore, moreover*
To change direction or show contrast:	*on the other hand, however, on the contrary, even though, nonetheless, conversely, but, yet*
To indicate time, place, or order:	*finally, first, next, then, further, meanwhile, above all, still, again*

Be Positive About Negatives

Multiple negatives create confusion.

> Snyder did not believe the lack of funding was unimportant.

Just what *did* Snyder believe? Make your reader's job easier by recasting the negatives in a positive form.

> Snyder believed the lack of funding was important.

If your sentence loses some of its punch when restated positively, find ways to reinject emphasis or drama.

> Snyder believed the lack of funding could be critical.

Double negatives can be ungrammatical (Don't do nothing illegal) or grammatical (The plan is not without merit). But even grammatical ones may be confusing.

not unaware = aware

Use double negatives sparingly and only when a positive statement fails to convey your meaning.

Misplaced negatives are also troublesome. Note the shift of meaning with the change in placement of "not" in the following example.

> **Misplaced:** It is <u>not</u> expected that tomorrow's speech will deal with the economy but will be confined to...

> **Correct:** It is expected that tomorrow's speech will <u>not</u> deal with the economy but will be confined to...

Review the use of negatives as you edit by looking for "not" and "un-." Is a sentence improved by changing negative to positive?

Using antonyms is a concise way to make negative statements positive.

> He did not pay attention to the request.
> He ignored the request.

> The office will not be open on Labor Day.
> The office will be closed on Labor Day.

They were not present during the interrogation.
They were absent during the interrogation.

Benzene is not safe to ingest.
Benzene is highly toxic.

Most words beginning with *in-* are negative: ineligible, inappropriate, inaudible. But some actually have positive meanings and should be used carefully: invaluable, inflammable, indebted, inhabitable.

And of course, double negatives can sometimes be fun.

I live in terror of not being misunderstood.—*Oscar Wilde*

5 First-Level Editing: Style

> A good style should show no sign of effort. What is written should seem like a happy accident.—*W. Somerset Maugham*

"Happy accidents" follow when you remove surplus words, avoid jargon and clichés, use words correctly, and choose vivid language.

Trim the Lard

Pruning extra words is one of the biggest jobs in editing. As you read each sentence, ask yourself which words could be dropped. Many of the guidelines presented in this book help tighten writing; the following suggestions for removing redundancies and padding will contribute to the goal.

Redundancies

Is your writing cluttered with words that have the same meaning (basic fundamentals, separate and distinct, near the vicinity of, exact same, reiterate again, various different, and general consensus of opinion)? Not all redundancies are so blatant. "In addition to...also" and "estimated at about... " are common ways of covering the same ground twice. Here are some others.

Redundant: The <u>age</u> of this tree is more than 1000 years <u>old</u>.
Trimmed: This tree is more than 1000 years old.

Redundant: His remarks were <u>limited only</u> to...
Trimmed: His remarks were limited to...

Redundant: An <u>additional</u> title was <u>added</u> to the list.
Trimmed: Another title was added to the list.

Redundant: The <u>reason</u> I'm late is <u>because</u> my car wouldn't start.
Trimmed: I'm late because my car wouldn't start.

Some expressions are not only repetitious but nonsensical. An "unsubstantiated rumor" suggests there could be a substantiated rumor. Writing "your own autobiography"—could you write anyone else's? Trim such excess words from your writing.

REDUNDANT EXPRESSIONS
(Delete the italicized words)

Adjectives
absolute necessity
active consideration
advance reservations
both alike
close proximity
complete monopoly
conclusive proof
end result
final outcome
free gift
general rule
new recruit
past history
personal opinion
positive identification
proposed plan
root cause
single unit
temporary reprieve
usual custom

Nouns
Capitol *building*
component *parts*
doctorate *degree*
weather *conditions*

Prepositional Phrases
brief *in duration*
classified *into groups*
estimated at *about*
few *in number*
filled *to capacity*
green *in color*
large *in size*
plan *in advance*
rectangular *in shape*
1 a.m. *in the morning*

Adverbs
completely surround
eliminate *entirely*
might *possibly*
mutually agreeable
really dangerous

Prefixes, Suffixes
*ir*regardless
to the west*ward*
*un*relentlessly

Verb Tails
assemble *together*
cancel *out*
connect *up*
continue *on*
enclosed *herein*
face *up to*
follow *after*
hurry *up*
join *together*
made *out* of
merge *together*
visit *with*

Repetitive Phrases
(Choose one part)
any and all
exact same
if and when
new all-time record high
unless and until

Padding

Make each word carry its own weight. "There is room in the basic unit for up to two disk drives" conveys no more than "The basic unit can hold two disk drives." "As of now we have no progress to report" starts with three clutter words.

Tightening windy expressions saves on printing, reduces reading time, and improves the likelihood that the document will actually be read. Here are some ways to streamline language.

PADDED:	TRIMMED:
a large (small) number of	many, few
ahead of schedule	early
along the lines of	like
at a later date	later
draw to your attention	show, point out
during the course of	during, while
had occasion to be	was
have need for	need
in advance of	before
in connection with	about
in regard (relation) to	about
make use of	use
not in a position to	unable to, cannot
on a regular basis	regularly
on two separate occasions	twice
put in an appearance	appeared
retain a position as	remain
such time as	when
take into consideration	consider
the majority of	most
until such time as	until

The following types of sentences are cluttered with too many words.

The...of

> The manufacture of paint is...
> Paint manufacture is...
>
> The level of crime
> The crime level

There are...who/that

> There are some circumstances that require...
> Some circumstances require...

It was/It is

> It was the Personnel Manager who issued the pink slips.
> The Personnel Manager issued the pink slips.
>
> It is necessary to sign...
> You need to (or must) sign...

Removing surplus words forces you to think about exactly what you want to say. Expressing your ideas more accurately may make total word count go up instead of down. That's all right. The goal is not simply to lop off words but to make all of them work for you.

> I believe more in the scissors
> than I do in the pencil.—*Truman Capote*

Know Your Words

The almost-right word is not good enough. "Deprecate" won't do if you mean "depreciate" or "prerequisite" if you mean "perquisite." A spell-checker won't keep you from using the wrong word, so make a habit of looking up meanings in a good dictionary. Read respected authors to develop a feeling for the correct use of words.

Ordinary words used precisely are more impressive than big words used sloppily. But even ordinary words can be used imprecisely. Do you write "always" when you should write "usually," "never" when "seldom" is more accurate, or "exactly" when "nearly" is a better word?

If you can't decide which of several words to use, try my method—put the alternatives in brackets. Later, when you return to the bracketed spot, the choice may be easier.

Commonly Misused Words

Affect/effect. *Affect* is primarily a verb, meaning to have an influence upon (How did the pills affect you?). *Effect* as a noun means result or consequence (The effect of the pills was easy to see); as a verb, it means to bring about (The pills effected a cure).

Aggravate. To make worse; not a substitute for *irritate* or *annoy*.

Anxious. Uneasy, apprehensive. Appropriate where apprehension or concern is implied; *eager* is the word to use when something is earnestly desired.

Claim. Many careful writers prefer the verbs *assert* or *maintain*.

Complement/compliment. These words have both noun and verb forms. *Complement* means to go well with or satisfy a need. *Compliment* means to praise.

Comprise. To include or be composed of. Avoid *is comprised of*; instead, use *comprises* or *consists of*.

> The whole comprises the parts.
> The parts constitute the whole.

Convince/persuade. *Convince* involves a state of mind (convince that), *persuade* a course of action (persuade to).

> She convinced me that the Earth is flat.
> He persuaded me to join the Flat Earth Society.

Dilemma. Use *dilemma* to indicate two choices, each undesirable. To describe a generally difficult situation, use *predicament*.

Equally. Use only where equality pertains.

> **Wrong:** The night shift performs equally as well as the day shift. (To correct the sentence, delete equally.)

> **Right:** The sum was divided equally among the heirs.

Farther/further. Use *farther* with physical distance. (He can see farther than I can.) To indicate extent or degree, use *further*. (Let's study the matter further.)

Fewer/less. Use *fewer* with things that can be counted (individual numbers or units); use *less* with quantity.

> Fewer mistakes, less embarrassment.

Fulsome. Means disgusting, excessive, insincere. Don't reach for this word when you mean plentiful.

Irregardless. Use *regardless* or *irrespective*, not this mixture of the two.

It's. Means *it is* or *it has*. The correct possessive pronoun is *its*. (See p. 92.)

Like/as. Use *like* with nouns or pronouns (She is tall, like her father). Use *as* with phrases (Profits rose, as in the previous quarter).

Literally. Means really or actually; don't use as an intensifier. Delete from a sentence like "He literally exploded when he heard the news."

Percentage. Avoid using as a substitute for *some*.

Preventive. Not *preventative*.

Principal. (1) An adjective meaning chief or main; (2) a noun designating a school official; (3) in a legal context, an important person. Often confused with *principle*, which is a rule or fundamental truth.

Respectively. Singly, in the order stated. The correct word in the complimentary close of a letter is *respectfully*.

-self. Correct if adding emphasis (I saw the Pope himself) or as a reflexive pronoun (She hurt herself). Not interchangeable with a pronoun.

Wrong: Riley and myself are heading the team.

Right: Riley and I are heading the team.

Suspicion. A noun, not a verb. You have a suspicion, or you suspect something, but you don't suspicion something.

That/which. Use *that* to introduce a restrictive clause and *which* to introduce a nonrestrictive or parenthetical one.

> Your manuscript is both good and original; but the part that is good is not original, and the part that is original is not good.—*Samuel Johnson*

> My decision, which didn't come easily, is final.

Unique. An overworked word, often misused for *rare* or *notable*.

Incorrect plurals are a common source of error. Words with Latin roots (*data, criteria, phenomena, media*) have irregular singular and plural forms: *phenomenon* (singular) and *phenomena* (plural). Since these words are not made plural by adding *s* or *es*, many people don't know whether they are using a singular or plural word. They make two kinds of mistakes:

- Using the plural form of the word when singular is called for

  Age was the sole criteria for determining eligibility. (Make that **criterion**.)

- Using a singular verb with a plural form of the word

  The media was excluded from the meeting. (Make that **were**.)

Add professional polish to your writing by using singular and plural words correctly. Refer to the "Irregular Plurals" list for help.

IRREGULAR PLURALS

Singular:	Plural:
alumna (fem.)	alumnae
alumnus (masc.)	alumni (masc. or both sexes)
analysis	analyses
antenna	antennas (radio, TV), antennae (insects)
apparatus	apparatus *or* apparatuses
appendix	appendixes *or* appendices
bacterium	bacteria
crisis	crises
criterion	criteria
curriculum	curricula *or* curriculums
genus	genera
index	indexes (publishing), indices (math)
kibbutz	kibbutzim
matrix	matrices *or* matrixes
medium	media
millennium	millennia
phenomenon	phenomena
radius	radii
stratum	strata
symposium	symposia *or* symposiums
synopsis	synopses
vertebra	vertebrae *or* vertebras

matrix + matrix = matrices

Cut Clichés and Hackneyed Expressions

Words that are overworked lose their force. When every event is a "crisis," it's hard to get worked up about another one.

Voguish words are a poor vehicle for fresh ideas; be wary of expressions that seem to appear, unbeckoned.

> Modern writing at its worst...consists in gumming together long strips of words which have already been set in order by someone else and making the results presentable by sheer humbug.
> —*George Orwell*

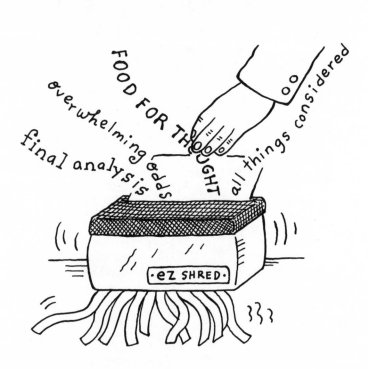

If an expression is both hackneyed and garbled, you are vulnerable to smirks or outright guffaws.

> Keep a stiff upper hand.
> Opening up a whole can of wax...
> Chafing at the bit...
> It created a human cry.
> They just shrugged their noses.
> He's a ragged individualist.

By avoiding clichés altogether, you appear more professional. Shun the expressions on the "Overworked Expressions" list.

OVERWORKED EXPRESSIONS

abreast of the times
add insult to injury
all things considered
along these lines
ample opportunity
as a matter of fact
at a loss for words
at long last
back burner
benefit of the doubt
better late than never
bitter end
bone of contention
by the same token
capacity crowd
checkered career
city fathers
considered opinion
controlling factor
crying need

drastic action
due consideration
eminently successful
equal to the occasion
exception that proves the
   rule
exercise in futility
existing conditions
festive occasion
few well-chosen words
final analysis
finishing touches
food for thought
force of circumstance
foregone conclusion
give the green light to
grave concern
heated argument
herculean efforts
inflationary spiral

continued on p. 76

OVERWORKED EXPRESSIONS

in no uncertain terms
in short supply
in this day and age
irreparable loss
it goes without saying
just desserts
keep options open
leave no stone unturned
leave well enough alone
lend a helping hand
long-felt need
marked contrast
moment of truth
more than meets the eye
narrow escape
needs no introduction
one and the same
on more than one occasion
open secret
other things being equal
overwhelming odds

own worst enemy
paramount importance
part and parcel
path of least resistance
regrettable incident
reliable source
remedy the situation
ripe old age
round of applause
second to none
select few
sweeping changes
too numerous to mention
unprecedented situation
untimely end
viable alternative
view with alarm
wave of the future
whole new ball game
you don't have to be a
  rocket scientist

Speak Out

Strive for assertive writing. It is direct and crisp, unburdened by the passive voice, lifeless verbs, and too many qualifiers.

> English is a remarkably clear, flexible, and useful language. We should use it in all of our communications.—*Daniel O'Neal, Jr.*
>
> Hear, hear!—*Jan Venolia*

Use the Active Voice

The passive voice combines a form of the verb *to be* with the past participle of another verb (was submitted, are seen, is urged, were reported, has been completed). When you write in the passive voice, the subject is acted upon.

Passive: The report was written by Molly McCoy.

In the active voice, subject of the sentence is the "doer."

Active: Molly McCoy wrote the report.

Each voice has legitimate uses. The passive voice is appropriate in the following circumstances:

- In technical writing

  The air is heated by being circulated over the coils.

- If the object of the action is more important than the subject

  The meeting was postponed.
  The veteran was awarded the Medal of Honor.

- If the subject is unknown

  The article was unsigned.
  Information was leaked to the press.
  Documents were stolen from the secured area.

- When you want to avoid naming a specific person

  The missing papers were returned.
  The time it takes to write a report is wasted if the report is not read.

But in general, the active voice should predominate. Notice how changing from passive to active voice makes the following sentence shorter and livelier.

Passive: It is recommended that special attention be paid to how productivity can be improved by introducing profit-sharing.

Who recommends, pays attention, and improves? We have to guess.

Active: Management should consider how profit-sharing can improve productivity.

Don't shift from active to passive voice mid-sentence.

Poor: Such a program costs little, and many are benefited by it.

Better: Such a program costs little and benefits many.

Avoid Lifeless Verbs
The *Associated Press Guide to Good Writing* points out the pomposity of the word *address* when used for something other than a letter: "Don't address a problem. Instead, deal with it, take it up, consider it, tackle it, cope with it." Good advice!

A lifeless verb brings a sentence to a standstill. *Exist, occur,* and forms of *to be* and *to have* are the worst offenders.

Poor: The Neighborhood Watch program exists in certain communities where there is concern about the crime rate.

Better: The Neighborhood Watch program reflects community concern about the crime rate.

It may seem strange to criticize a verb as essential as *to be*. But sentences built on *to be* are frequently heavy with accompanying baggage.

> The purpose of the report is to provide a means of comparing sales in the four regions.
>
> The report compares sales in the four regions.

> Cutting government spending is another way to reduce the deficit.
>
> Cutting government spending also reduces the deficit.

> X is different from Y.
>
> X differs from Y.

Lifeless verbs are often noun-heavy. When *indicates* becomes *is an indication of*, and *knows* becomes *has a knowledge of*, the pace slows down. Look for word endings like *-ment*, *-tion*, *-ity*, *-ance*, and *-ness*, and give them a shot of adrenaline.

LIFELESS:	LIVELY:
a preference for	prefer
present suggestions for avoiding	suggest ways to avoid
There is a belief among the reporters	The reporters believe
Their response was an indication of	Their response indicated
has a tendency to	tends to

Don't Overqualify

Too many qualifiers weaken writing. E. B. White dramatically described such words as *rather*, *very*, *little*, and *pretty* as "leeches that infest the pond of prose, sucking the blood of words." No hedging there!

Omit qualifiers that diminish your ideas or are inherently contradictory:

> rather important
> more perfect
> somewhat irresponsible
> almost unique
> very fatal
> moderately exhaustive

Replace qualifiers that just intensify meaning with more descriptive words:

> very important = critical, crucial, central
> really angry = outraged, furious

or just delete them:

> very obstinate = obstinate
> utterly reject = reject
> very ecstatic = ecstatic

Jettison Jargon

Jargon that is the specialized language of a particular science or trade has its proper place. It's an efficient shorthand when writing for an audience that speaks the language.

But some writers use pseudo-technical words simply to impress the reader or to create a verbal smokescreen. Here are the symptoms of such gobbledygook:

- Passive voice

- Prepositional phrases

- Piled-up nouns

- Converted parts of speech

- Abstractions and empty terms

- Buzz words

A murky **passive voice** predominates in jargon-heavy writing. We find neither subject nor actor, just the action: conclusions are reached, relations are improved, and problems are anticipated. (See p. 77.)

Prepositional phrases, unending and uninteresting, often provide the framework of a gobbledygook sentence.

> **Poor:** The root of the problem of negotiation, in which there is the interaction of representatives of groups with conflicting points of view, is the taking of adversarial positions from which retreat is difficult.

> **Better:** When individuals who represent groups with conflicting opinions act as adversaries, retreat from their positions is difficult.

Piled-up nouns proliferate in writing that is full of jargon.

> systems modification effort
> employee productivity improvement possibilities
> highway litter reduction program
> damage situation
> disabled student learning environment

Parts of speech are converted into other parts of speech. Verbs become nouns:

America is on the improve.

Even more often, nouns become verbs:

The design was prototyped into a working model.

We're going to incentivize these people by multiyearing their program.

It appears there isn't a noun that can't be verbed!

Abstractions and empty terms disguise real meaning. Under the mistaken impression that something obscure is profound and that complexity has clout, writers stifle their natural style. They don't write "We tested it and it works," but "During the course of the above referenced investigation, data were developed and subjected to rigorous computer modeling which suggest that the system will, within specified parameters, produce viable results."

The first step in getting readers to pay attention to what we're writing is to pay attention ourselves. Too often we regurgitate phrases without having digested their meaning ("decisional significance"). We use high-sounding words for the sake of being high-sounding—or to avoid being direct.

The income derived from the revenue enhancement program will be allocated to revitalizing the nation's infrastructure.

Translation: The gasoline tax will pay for repairing our highways and sewer systems.

In jargon-laden writing, **buzz words** abound. Many are legitimate words that overuse has turned into clichés (viable, image, dialogue, disseminate, implement, relate). Some are legitimate words in certain contexts but their popular usage tends to be incorrect (parameter, modality, metaphor). Some have minimal claim to legitimacy (finalize, learning experience, out years, throughput, taxwise).

> A good catchword can obscure analysis
> for fifty years.—*Wendell L. Wilkie*

Evoke Images

Our language is rich with graphic words.

bamboo curtain
the big bang
bottleneck

domino theory
grass-roots campaign
linear thinking

These words appeal to the senses; they help the reader visualize and remember. Yet writers are sometimes unaware of the imagery they are using. Their images reveal fuzzy thinking.

His Achilles' heel was his weak knee.

This field of research is so virginal that no human eye has ever set foot in it. (found in a Ph.D. dissertation)

Keep your images under control. The more aware you are of the pictures words make, the better you will use them. Here's how a master does it.

Sending men to that Army is like shoveling fleas across a barnyard—not half of them get there.—*Abraham Lincoln*

Metaphors are a technique for creating images. Unlike Lincoln's simile above, which makes a comparison using the word *like*, metaphors compare directly.

Bureaucracy is a giant mechanism operated by pygmies. —*Honoré de Balzac*

A good metaphor is transparent; it enhances meaning without drawing attention to itself. Overusing such figures of speech diminishes their effectiveness; in small doses, they are an artful device.

> How infinite is the debt owed to metaphors
> by politicians who want to speak strongly
> but are not sure what they are going to say.
> —*Winston Churchill*

Watch Small Words

Small words, if misused, can create big problems. Check whether you have used the following small words correctly.

A, an, the. Incorrect use of the articles *a* and *the* can alter meaning. Notice the difference when *the* is omitted.

> The more specific details you provide...
> The more specific the details you provide...

The first emphasizes the quantity of specific details; the second, how specific those details are. Either could be correct, so you should choose the one that's closer to your meaning.

The beginning sound of the next word determines whether you use *a* or *an*. A consonant sound (which is not necessarily a consonant) is preceded by *a*, a vowel sound by *an*.

> a uniform, *but* an unprecedented
> a European, *but* an Easterner
> a history, *but* an hour
> a one-dollar bill, *but* an only child

Uniform and *European* are pronounced as if they began with the letter y, so *a* is the correct article to use with them. The *h* in *history* is pronounced, so it requires *a*. The *h* in *hour* is silent, calling for *an*. *One* is pronounced as if it begins with *w*, whereas the initial sound of *only* is *o*.

The choice of article to precede initials and acronyms is another trap for unwary writers. Again, it is how the word is pronounced that matters. Do you pronounce the letters individually (SEC lawyer, NBA player)? If so, do they sound as if they begin with a vowel or a consonant? "S" sounds as if it were spelled "ess" and "N" as if it were "en." With both of those acronyms, you should use *an*.

Is the acronym pronounced as a word? Then use the article *a* if it's pronounced with a consonant sound (a NATO official), or *an* if it has a vowel sound (an OSHA ruling).

Like, as. Use *like* in direct comparisons of nouns.

> Hell hath no fury like a bureaucrat scorned.—*Milton Friedman*

> Nothing recedes like success.—*Walter Winchell*

Use *as* when the comparison involves verbs.

> Do as I do.
> He resented the implication, as anyone would.

Etc. Relying on *etc.* at the end of a series of items suggests that you are either lazy or uncertain about what else to include. Indicate incompleteness by writing *such as* (or *such...as*) ahead of examples.

> A well-stocked library will include such authors as...
> The event produced additional sources of income, such as...

's. Errors of agreement with the contraction *'s* are so common that it's probably smart to scrutinize each use of the apostrophe. *It's, there's, here's,* and *that's* are ALWAYS contractions, usually of the word *is*: *it is, there is, here is,* and *that is*. The word *is* is singular. Most people know this, yet they make the mistake of treating the contraction of *is* as a plural. Though they would never write "There is three reasons," they might let "There's three reasons" slip by. Expand contractions to see if they harbor the word *is*. If they do, and you need a plural verb, use *are*. "There are three reasons."

It's is probably the most misused word in American writing. Since the apostrophe is one way to show possession, it may seem logical to use one when making the word *it* possessive. But *its* is already possessive. The only time you need to add an apostrophe is when the word is a contraction of *it is* or *it has*.

> It's a question that suggests its answer.

it's = it is or it has

Reading good writing is an excellent way to absorb the rules discussed in this chapter. How do these authors handle language? Reading the best classical and modern writers will give you more insight into ways to use words effectively than you will get from reading about good writing—and it's a lot more fun.

6 Second-Level Editing: Punctuation

> Word carpentry is like any other kind of
> carpentry. You must join your sentences
> smoothly.—*Anatole France*

Punctuation marks are road signs to help the reader: Slow down, detour, stop. Too much punctuation makes writing choppy, too little creates confusion. Its purpose is to clarify meaning, not erect roadblocks, so use it with that in mind.

Apostrophes

Apostrophes primarily show possession or a contraction; they are also used with certain plurals.

Use an apostrophe to show possession, as follows:

- With all singular words, add 's.

  the jury's verdict
  the twin's room (one person)
  the witness's testimony
  Jane Nelson's job

- With all plural words that end in *s*, add the apostrophe only.

  teachers' conference
  the twins' mother
  the witnesses' testimony
  the Nelsons' house

- With plural words that don't end in *s*, add *'s*.

  children's toys
  men's room
  women's issues

When you want the final *sis* or *siz* sound to be pronounced, add *'s* rather than just the apostrophe.

  Marx's philosophy

To avoid such common errors as "the Nelson's house," first make the word plural (Nelsons), then add the apostrophe to make it possessive (Nelsons').

When making a phrase or compound noun possessive, add 's to the last word.

> my brother-in-law's Lexus
> the Surgeon General's warning
> the senator from Maine's vote

However, making a phrase possessive can get out of hand.

> **Poor:** the officer who resigned last week's signature
> **Better:** the signature of the officer who resigned last week

When there is joint ownership of a single item, add 's to the last name only: Laura and Tom's car (one car). When the ownership is not joint, add 's to each name: Laura's and Tom's cars (two cars).

Apostrophes are often omitted in names of organizations, institutions or countries that end in s, where the words are more descriptive than possessive.

> Teachers College
> Consumers Union
> Publishers Weekly
> United Nations delegate

Apostrophes are usually—but not always—used in organization names that do not end in s.

> Longshoremen's Union
> McDonald's
> *but* Childrens Hospital *or* Children's Hospital

Find a reasonably reliable source of information about a given name (letterhead, web site, phonebook) and use that form.

Use an apostrophe to show a contraction or omission.

can't (cannot)
haven't (have not)
it's (it is)
ma'am (madam)
o'clock (of the clock)
Spirit of '76
there's (there is)
won't (will not)

Be awful nice to 'em going up, because you're gonna meet 'em all comin' down.—*Jimmy Durante*

Note: *It's* is a contraction of *it is* or *it has*; *its* (without the apostrophe) is a possessive pronoun.

Contraction: It's not the men in my life that counts—it's the life in my men.—*Mae West*

Possession: There is more to life than increasing its speed. —*Mohandas K. Gandhi*

Use an apostrophe to show duration.

one minute's delay
two weeks' vacation
ten years' experience

Use an apostrophe where needed for clarity and with certain plurals.

    2x4's
    C.O.D.'s
    do's and don'ts
    M.D.'s
    Ph.D.'s
    p's and q's

    There are two c's in accumulate.
    Her report card had 3 A's.

However, plurals are usually shown not by adding an apostrophe but just by adding *s* or *es*.

Don't use apostrophes in the following cases:

	WRONG:	RIGHT:
	CD's	CDs
keeping up with the Jones's		keeping up with the Joneses
	one's and two's	ones and twos
	"The Red Pony" 's ending	the ending of "The Red Pony"
	the Roaring '20's	the Roaring '20s *or* Twenties

Colons

Colons have two main jobs: to introduce something that follows, and to provide separation (as in ratios). Capitalize the first word after a colon if it begins a complete sentence.

Use a colon to introduce something.

The difference between intelligence and education is this: Intelligence will make you a good living.—*Charles F. Kettering*

The results of the survey may be summarized as follows: in favor of rezoning, 59%; opposed, 41%.

Carney's Law: There's at least a 50-50 chance that someone will print the name Craney incorrectly.—*Jim Canrey*

Use a colon to separate certain words or numbers.

Kids Write Right! (Berkeley: Tricycle Press, 2000)
Congressional Directory, Washington: U.S. Government
    Printing Office
12:30 p.m.
Matthew 6:3-7
Nature 3:127-9
Dear Ms. Fortune:
a ratio of 2:1
proportions of 5:3:1

Don't use a colon to introduce words that would fit smoothly into the sentence without the colon.

Wrong: Lewis Carroll defines arithmetic as: ambition, distraction, uglification, and derision.

Right: Lewis Carroll defines arithmetic as ambition, distraction...

Wrong: The effects of the reorganization are: an increase in productivity and a reduction in absenteeism and personnel turnover.

Right: The effects of the reorganization are an increase...

Don't use a colon when the word "follows" or "following" does not immediately precede whatever is listed.

Wrong: A list of those attending follows. Notice that management and labor are both represented:
    Jack Johnson
    Laurel Ann Schmidt
    Robin Reynolds

Right: A list of those attending follows. Notice that management and labor are both represented.
    Jack Johnson
    Laurel Ann Schmidt
    Robin Reynolds

Commas

Commas prevent misreading and clarify meaning. However, unnecessary commas are a distraction, so add only those that promote ease of reading.

Use a comma in the following:

- In compound sentences, to separate independent clauses

  I did not attend his funeral, but I wrote a nice letter saying I approved it.—*Mark Twain*

  Opportunities are usually disguised as hard work, so most people don't recognize them.—*Ann Landers*

- With nonrestrictive clauses

  The law, in its majestic equality, forbids the rich as well as the poor to sleep under bridges.—*Anatole France*

- Following participial phrases

  Thrusting my nose firmly between his teeth, I threw him heavily to the ground on top of me.—*Mark Twain*

- To indicate a pause or break in continuity

  A bore is a man who, when you ask him how he is, tells you. —*Bert Taylor*

- When addressing someone directly

  Depend upon it, sir, when a man knows he is to be hanged in a fortnight, it concentrates his mind wonderfully.—*Samuel Johnson*

- With appositives

  George Bernard Shaw, the Irish-born playwright and social critic, thought the lack of money was the root of all evil.

- With coordinate adjectives

  a tall, stately redwood
  the slow, relentless pace

  I found him a plausible, attractive rogue, all nervous energy and wit.—*Thomas Flanagan*

- With complementary or contrasting elements

  Skepticism, like chastity, should not be relinquished too readily.—*George Santayana*

  Grub first, then ethics.—*Bertolt Brecht*

- Following introductory phrases

  In the main, opera in English is just about as sensible as baseball in Italian.—*H. L. Mencken*

- In a series

  Talk low, talk slow, and don't say too much.—*John Wayne*

Note: Some consider the final comma in a series to be optional. However, by always adding the final comma, you avoid potential confusion.

  Unclear: Two developments will affect pregnancy, birth and infants.

  Clear: Two developments will affect pregnancy, birth, and infants.

- For clarity

  Even though I was young when she told me that, I understood her meaning perfectly.

  Everybody is ignorant, only on different subjects.—*Will Rogers*

  If she chooses, Adams can apply for an extension.

- With identical words or unrelated numbers

  If such a tragedy had happened to you, you would understand.

  No matter how thin you slice it, it's still baloney.—*Alfred E. Smith*

  Total enrollment is 24, 15 of whom hold advanced degrees.

- To show omission

  You are apprehensive of monarchy; I, of aristocracy.—*John Adams*

- With quotations

  Billy Rose said, "Never invest your money in anything that eats or needs repairing."

  "My goose," the chef said, "is cooked."

- When the modifier follows the modified

  The shareholders' meeting, upbeat and constructive, lasted four hours.

- With titles

  Warren Williams, Jr.
  Drew Hoffmann, Attorney at Law
  Stephanie Peabody, M.D.
  Justin Adams, Management Consultant

- Following opening subordinate clauses

  If all economists were laid end to end, they would not reach a conclusion.—*George Bernard Shaw*

- With parenthetical expressions

  It requires an unusual mind, according to Alfred North Whitehead, to analyze the obvious.

  Prophecy, however honest, is generally a poor substitute for experience.—*Justice Benjamin N. Cardozo*

Don't use commas in the following cases:

- Between short, closely related clauses

  Some carve great careers while others simply chisel.
  —*Laurence J. Peter*

- Between an independent and a dependent clause

  Finance is the art of passing currency from hand
  independent clause
  to hand until it finally disappears.—*Robert Sarnoff*
  dependent clause

  Don't talk unless you can improve the silence.—*Vermont proverb*

- With restrictive clauses

  Men who have a pierced ear are better prepared
  restrictive clause
  for marriage; they buy jewelry and they've experienced pain.—*Rita Rudner*

  An optimist is a driver who thinks that an empty space at the curb won't have a fire hydrant beside it.

- Following the last item in a series

  His reports occasionally lapse into disorganized, incoherent, jargon-filled writing. (*not* jargon-filled, writing)

- Between adjectives where the first modifies both the second adjective and the noun

  illegal campaign contributions
  a snowy Christmas eve

Dashes

Dashes are an interruption, like waving your finger under the reader's nose. Whenever a colon, semicolon, or comma would serve just as well, use it. Reserve the dash for situations where dramatic emphasis is justified.

Use a dash in the following cases:

- To emphasize what follows

  Familiarity breeds contempt—and children.—*Mark Twain*

  When I was six I made my mother a little hat—out of her new blouse.—*Lilly Daché*

- To indicate an abrupt change or an afterthought

  The business of government is to keep the government out of business—that is, unless business needs government aid.
  —*Will Rogers*

  The best way to keep children home is to make the home atmosphere pleasant—and let the air out of the tires.—*Dorothy Parker*

- To summarize or explain

  The principle of give and take is the principle of diplomacy—give one and take ten.—*Mark Twain*

> A pedestrian is a man who has two cars—one being driven by his wife, the other by one of his children.—*Robert Benchley*

Dashes can be combined with exclamation marks, question marks, and quotation marks.

> Her response was emphatic—"I will not sign this!"

But don't combine one dash with a comma.

> **Wrong:** The books—all 12 of them, were overdue.

> **Right:** The books—all 12 of them—were overdue.

Word processors provide both an em dash (—) and an en dash (–). The above examples call for an em dash. The en dash is primarily used to indicate inclusiveness.

> 1988–89
> pp. 35–47
> New York–Boston train

A 2-em dash indicates omitted letters (Ms. T——, D——d right!). A 3-em dash replaces entire words, as in a bibliography where it is used instead of repeating an author's name.

On a standard typewriter keyboard, use two hyphens for an em dash and one hyphen for an en dash.

Exclamation Points

Exclamation points provide a punchy ending. Use exclamation points after interjections:

> Ouch!

after exclamatory sentences:

> That hurt!

and after imperative sentences that indicate strong feelings:

> Don't step on my toe again!

Too many exclamation points leave a reader feeling punched out, so save them for just a few important places.

Hyphens

Hyphens divide words at the end of the line (see Word Division, p. 162) and join certain words to form compounds (break-in, old-fashioned music).

Hyphenate a few prefixes.

anti-hero
ex-husband
post-mortem

Today, most prefixes are not hyphenated.

bipartisan
infrastructure
interrelated
macroeconomics
microorganism
millisecond
multitasking
nanotechnology
preempt
reenter
semiconductor

However, retain the hyphen in the following cases:

- When confusion or an awkward pronunciation results from the one-word form

co-owner
re-read
co-opt
un-ionized
co-worker

- When the root word is capitalized

sub-Saharan
pro-Israeli

pre-Columbian
post-World War I

- When the second part of a hyphenated term consists of two or more words

non-tumor-bearing tissue
post-20th-century inventions
pre-gold-strike era
ultra-high-speed device

- When certain double or triple letters would occur

anti-intellectual
non-native
semi-independent
shell-like

Hyphenate fractions and compound numbers.

one-third
forty-seven

Hyphenate to combine a numeral and noun or adjective (a unit modifier).

$1/2$-acre lot
10-kilometer run
5-ml beaker
50-odd members
75-page report

Hyphenate certain compounds.

Your meaning determines whether to hyphenate a compound

word. An *old film buff* describes an elderly person who enjoys movies. An *old-film buff* is someone who enjoys old films.

Hyphenate to prevent misreading in such cases as the following.

Adjectives

> bricks-and-mortar bookstore
> dog-eared book
> double-decker bus
> economy-sized package
> fast-talking salesperson
> good-natured response
> in-house memo
> just-in-time inventory
> long-term effects
> revolving-door policy
> stiff-necked attitude
> thought-provoking statement
> time-honored custom

> The best mind-altering drug is truth.—*Lily Tomlin*

> Brevity is only skin deep, and the world is full of thin-skinned people.—*Richard Armour*

Nouns

> break-in
> go-between
> know-how
> ne'er-do-well
> page-turner

poet-humorist
well-wisher
write-off

There are no whole truths; all truths are half-truths.—*Alfred North Whitehead*

Improvised Compounds

dog-eat-dog
do-it-yourself
Johnny-come-lately
stick-to-itiveness
topsy-turvy
touch-me-not

Nowadays people are divided into three classes—the Haves, the Have-nots, and the Have-Not-Paid-for-What-They-Haves.—*Earl Wilson*

Omit hyphens in established compounds when they are not needed to clarify meaning.

city hall news
high school dropout
real estate office
White House staff

See p. 172 for a more complete discussion of the formation of compound words.

Don't use hyphens in the following cases:

antiwar
bilateral

catlike
coordinate
midtown
overanxious
postdoctoral
statewide
transcontinental
underfunded

Never hyphenate a word ending in *-ly*.

Wrong: widely-known author, commonly-held assumption, publicly-held stock

Right: widely known author, commonly held assumption, publicly held stock

Parentheses

Parentheses have the effect of an aside, as if you were trying to say the words behind your hand. Use them only now and then or your writing will lack directness.

Use parentheses to set off an explanation or to add information.

The teacher (who chose not to reveal his identity) submitted a list of the crazy excuses he'd received for late homework.

When the parentheses contain a complete statement or question, put the closing punctuation mark inside the final parenthesis.

(She is the shortstop.)
(Was he dreaming?)

Periods

Periods are used at the ends of sentences and abbreviations. In the UK, the period is called a "full stop," which is a good description of what it does.

Use a period as follows:

- At the end of a declarative sentence (a statement)

  Artificial intelligence is no match for natural stupidity.

- At the end of an imperative sentence (instructions, requests, orders)

  Get your facts first. Then you can distort them as you please.—*Mark Twain*

- With some abbreviations and initials

  p.m.
  Mr./Ms./Mrs.
  vs.
  etc.
  J. F. Kennedy, *but* JFK (no periods)

If an abbreviation ends a sentence, don't add a second period.

  We will expect you at 10 a.m.

An *ellipsis* consists of three periods. It is used to show an omission within quoted material.

  A great many people have...asked how I manage to get so much work done and still keep looking so dissipated. —*Robert Benchley*

If the ellipsis *follows* the period that ends a sentence, put a space between that period and the ellipses.

> The only way to get rid of temptation is to yield to it. ...I can resist everything but temptation.—*Oscar Wilde*

If the ellipsis *precedes* the period that ends a sentence, use four evenly spaced periods.

> An important scientific innovation rarely makes its way by gradually winning over and converting its opponents.... What does happen is that its opponents gradually die out. —*Max Planck*

Question Marks

Put a question mark after a direct question (in other words, at the end of an interrogative sentence).

> Did you check out the web site?
> Who is preparing the report?

Do not use a question mark with an indirect question or polite request.

> He asked who is making the reservation.
> Will you please close the door as you leave.

Quotation Marks

Quotation marks have several jobs.

- To enclose titles of short pieces (songs, poems, articles, short stories)

> Do you know the words to "The Star-Spangled Banner"?

- To set words or phrases apart from the surrounding text

  When the government talks about "raising capital," it means printing it.—*Peter Drucker*

  The package was marked "Refused—Return to Sender."

  I prefer the word "homemaker" because "housewife" implies that there may be a wife someplace else.—*Bella Abzug*

  The bride and groom said their "I do's."

- As a substitute for the words *so-called*

  The "error" identified by the grammar-checker was actually correct.

- To indicate spoken words

  Victor Borge said, "Laughter is the shortest distance between two people."

  Diplomacy is the art of saying "Nice doggie!" till you can find a rock.—*Wynn Catlin*

Single quotation marks enclose quoted material within a quotation.

  Richard Armour quipped, "That money talks I'll not deny. I heard it once: It said, 'Goodbye.'"

  Kin Hubbard asked, "Why don't th' feller who says, 'I'm not a speechmaker,' let it go at that instead of giving a demonstration?"

Punctuate quoted material as follows:

- Place periods and commas inside the closing quotation mark.

  "Money won't buy happiness," according to Bill Vaughan, "but it will pay the salaries of a large research staff to study the problem."

- Place all other punctuation marks outside the closing quotation mark, unless they are part of what is quoted.

  He shouted, "May Day! May Day!"

  Did you hear them calling "Help"?

  Thoreau asked the question, "What is the use of a house if you haven't got a tolerable planet to put it on?"

Semicolons

> There is almost always a greater pleasure to come across a semicolon than a period....You get a pleasant feeling of expectancy; there is more to come; read on; it will get clearer.—*George R. Will*

The semicolon produces a more emphatic break than a comma. Use semicolons when you want a stronger pause than a comma but less separation than two sentences.

Use a semicolon between independent clauses.

Beware of little expenses; a small leak will sink a great ship. —*Benjamin Franklin*

The brain is a wonderful organ; it starts working the moment you get up in the morning and doesn't stop until you get to the office.—*Robert Frost*

Hanging is too good for a man who makes puns; he should be drawn and quoted.—*Fred Allen*

One friend in a lifetime is much; two are many; three are hardly possible.—*Henry Adams*

I'm not a vegetarian because I love animals; I'm a vegetarian because I hate plants.—*A. Whitney Brown*

Use a semicolon between items in a series that contains commas.

If a man runs after money, he's money-mad; if he keeps it, he's a capitalist; if he spends it, he's a playboy; if he doesn't get it, he's a ne'er-do-well; if he doesn't try to get it, he lacks ambition. If he gets it without working for it, he's a parasite; and if he accumulates it after a lifetime of hard work, people call him a fool who never got anything out of life.
—*Vic Oliver*

Don't use a semicolon between an independent clause and a dependent (or subordinate) clause.

Wrong: The project will not be funded; even though it is worthwhile.

Right: The project will not be funded even though it is worthwhile.

7 Second-Level Editing: Grammar

> Grammar, rhetoric, and logic enrich enormously the phenomenon of being alive.—*George Santayana*

Good grammar is transparent. Instead of getting in the way, it helps readers understand what is written.

Most people use grammatical rules without being aware of them. But occasionally a question comes up: Should a verb be singular or plural? Which pronoun should I use: *I, me,* or *myself; who* or *whom*? Knowing the rules (or where to find them) answers such questions.

This section covers the six areas where most grammatical questions arise: agreement, pronouns, adjectives and adverbs, verbs, parallel structure, and no-fault sentences. Use these guidelines to sharpen your awareness of potential problems. The examples and rules will help you detect and correct errors.

Agreement
Every part of a sentence should agree with every related part. If you translate this rule into everyday English, you find it's saying something like this:

- Use singular verbs with singular subjects and plural verbs with plural subjects.

- Make a pronoun singular if its antecedent is singular and plural if the antecedent is plural.

Let's look at those two areas: subject/verb and antecedent/pronoun.

Make subject and verb agree in number.
A singular subject requires a singular verb.

> The wastepaper <u>basket</u> <u>is</u> a writer's best friend.
>   sing.   sing.
>   subj.   verb
> —*Isaac Bashevis Singer*

A plural subject requires a plural verb.

We are confronted with insurmountable opportunities.
pl. subj.   pl. verb
—Pogo (Walt Kelly)

The verb must also agree with the subject when the subject follows the verb.

What are the answers?
There is one doctor.
Answering questions from the press were three candidates.

Behind the phony tinsel of Hollywood lies the real tinsel.
—Oscar Levant

A compound subject joined by *and* requires a plural verb (a compound subject consists of two or more elements).

The rich man and his daughter are soon parted.
compound subject   pl. verb
—Kin Hubbard

Completing the form and mailing it promptly are both important.

Only presidents, editors, and people with tapeworms have the right to use the editorial "we."*—Mark Twain*

A compound subject joined by *or* or *nor* takes a singular verb.

A passport or tourist card is necessary.

If a compound subject is treated as a unit, it takes a singular verb.

Find and Replace is a useful word-processing function.
Baxter & Grand is a national accounting firm.

A compound subject preceded by the word *each* or *every* is singular.

Each question and answer was carefully considered.
Every representative and senator is on our mailing list.

When *as well as* precedes a word or phrase, it does not affect the number of the verb.

The owner, as well as his employees, is implicated.

In *either/or* and *neither/nor* constructions, the verb agrees with the nearest noun.

Either the equipment or the <u>samples</u> <u>were</u> contaminated.
plural subj. plural verb

Neither envelopes nor <u>letterhead</u> <u>was</u> delivered.
sing. subj.   sing. verb

The number of the verb is not affected by intervening phrases.

Working conditions, a subject of frequent debate, are...
The briefcase with the missing reports is...
The verb in the main clause of each of these examples is...
The verbs in each sentence are...
One in every ten components is...

Treat the following indefinite pronouns as singular: each, each one, every, everyone, everybody, either, neither, nobody, no one, any, anyone, anybody, somebody, someone.

In the United States there is more space where nobody is than where anybody is.—*Gertrude Stein*

However, when *each* follows a plural subject, the verb is plural.

> The teachers each have different ideas for solving the problem.

Treat the following indefinite pronouns either as singular or plural, depending on the context or meaning: none, some, more, all, most, half.

> All's fair in love and war.—*Francis Edward Smedley*

> All want to be learned, but none is willing to pay the price.
> —*Juvenal*

> More is experienced in one day in the life of a learned man than in the whole lifetime of an ignorant man.—*Seneca*

> More are experienced programmers than in previous years.

The word *number* is singular when preceded by *the*, plural when preceded by *a*.

> The number of mistakes was small.
> A number of mistakes were made.

Collective nouns (such as family, group, committee, couple, team, personnel, staff, majority) are singular unless they refer to individuals within the group.

> The personnel were screened for verbal and mathematical aptitudes. *(Individuals within the group were screened.)*

> The team was late. *(The group is treated as a unit.)*

> The contents of the test tube was withdrawn. *(as a whole)*

The contents of the package were examined. *(as individual elements)*

A subject that expresses a sum, rate, measurement, or quantity as a unit takes a singular verb even if the subject is plural.

Three centimeters is more than one inch.
Five dollars is a reasonable price.

Some words ending in *s* appear to be plural but are actually a singular concept: news, physics, economics, series, summons.

The news is good.
The series of tests was completed.

Handle relative pronouns (*who, which, that, what*) as follows:

- *Who, which,* and *that* take singular verbs when referring to singular words, plural verbs when referring to plural words.

  Singular: Anyone who hates children and dogs can't be all bad.—*W. C. Fields*

  Plural: People who bite the hand that feeds them usually lick the boot that kicks them.—*Eric Hoffer*

- *What* takes a singular verb, unless it has a plural antecedent.

  What kills a skunk is the publicity it gives itself.—*Abraham Lincoln*

Agreement should be between verb and subject, not between verb and complement.

The solution is strong locks.
subject   verb   complement

When the subject is a phrase or clause, use a singular verb.

Freedom of the press is limited to those who own one.
subject
—*A. J. Liebling*

Certain Latin words are the source of errors of agreement (*phenomena, criteria*). The table on p. 73 shows which words have retained their Latin plurals and which have been Anglicized.

Make pronoun and antecedent agree in number.

All <u>employees</u> must provide <u>their</u> own tools.

He is a self-made <u>man</u> and worships <u>his</u> creator.—*William Cowper*

Whatever <u>women</u> do <u>they</u> must do twice as well as men to be thought half as good. Luckily, this is not difficult. —*Charlotte Whitton*

When the <u>jury</u> returns to give <u>its</u> verdict...

Neither <u>Karen</u> nor <u>Linda</u> would break <u>her</u> silence. (Compounds joined by *or* or *nor* are singular.)

<u>Men</u> are never so tired and harassed as when <u>they</u> have to deal with a woman who wants a raise.—*Michael Korda*

The <u>tongue</u> weighs almost nothing, yet few people can hold <u>it</u>.

Pronouns
Use the correct case of pronouns.

Nominative	Possessive	Objective
I	my	me
you	your, yours	you
he	his	him
she	her, hers	her
it	its	it
we	our, ours	us
they	their, theirs	them
who	whose	whom

Use the nominative case when the pronoun is the subject.

> People <u>who</u> say <u>they</u> sleep like a baby usually don't have one.—*Leo Burke*
> (**Who** is the subject of the verb *say;* **they** is the subject of the verb *sleep.*)

> Wilson and I will attend.

Use the objective case when the pronoun is the object of a verb or preposition.

> Marriage is the alliance of two people, one of <u>whom</u> never remembers birthdays and the other never forgets <u>them</u>. —*Ogden Nash*
> (**Whom** is the object of the preposition *of;* **them** is the object of the verb *forgets.*)

> Submit the report to Wilson and me.

Use the possessive case when you want to show ownership.

> I should have the courage of my lack of conviction.—*Tom Stoppard*

> Wilson and Gaines missed their flight.

Once you've determined the correct case, you know which pronoun to use (for example, *I* or *me*, *who* or *whom*). The choice is easier if you mentally eliminate everything between the verb or preposition and the pronoun whose case you're trying to determine. Try it in the following example.

Wrong: The contest has narrowed down to [you and] I.

Right: The contest has narrowed down to you and me.

When in doubt about *who* or *whom*, substitute a pronoun for the word. If a nominative pronoun feels right (*I*, *we*, *she*), use *who* (the nominative form of the word). If an objective

pronoun fits (*me, us, her*), use *whom* (the objective form of the word).

> The first person who answers all questions correctly... (***she*** answers all questions...)

> The woman whom we hired has an MBA. (we hired ***her***)

Even though the word *whoever* follows the preposition *for* in the following example, its role as subject of the verb *had* in the dependent clause "whoever had jobs" determines the case.

> **Wrong:** They worked for whomever had jobs.

> **Right:** They worked for whoever had jobs.

If a pronoun follows *than* or *as*, mentally insert the missing verbs to determine the correct case. (The missing words are in parentheses in the following examples.)

> I am as hard-working as he (is).

> The supervisor corrects Smith more often than (she corrects) me.

> The supervisor corrects Smith more often than I (do).

Avoid unnecessary reflexive or intensive pronouns (pronouns ending in *-self* or *-selves*).

> **Wrong:** The summons was received by my partner and myself.
> **Right:** The summons was received by my partner and me.

> **Wrong:** My partner and myself received...
> **Right:** My partner and I received...

A reflexive pronoun is correctly used only when it refers back to the subject (*He injured himself*), and an intensive pronoun is used strictly for emphasis (*I will present the award myself*).

Make pronouns refer clearly to their antecedents.

A pronoun is a stand-in; the word or group of words it stands in for is called its antecedent. A reader should have no doubt about what antecedent a pronoun replaces.

<u>Celeste</u> gave the valet <u>her</u> car keys.
antecedent   pronoun

Ambiguous pronouns create confusion.

Unclear: She told her that her secretary had typed her resignation. *(Whose secretary? Whose resignation?)*

Unclear: Company A is losing sales to Company B and its competitors. *(Whose competitors, A's or B's?)*

Sometimes the antecedent is missing entirely.

Unclear: When you calculate the number of managers and subordinates, <u>it</u> is eye-opening. *(What does it refer to? Probably the ratio of managers to subordinates, which appears in the sentence only indirectly.)*

Clear: When you calculate the number of managers and subordinates, the ratio is eye-opening.

Adjectives and Adverbs

Use adjectives to modify nouns or pronouns; use adverbs to modify verbs, adjectives, or other adverbs.

The following examples illustrate correct usage.

She gave a <u>quick</u> answer. *(adj., modifies the noun **answer**; it describes what kind of answer)*

She answered <u>quickly.</u> *(adv., modifies the verb **answer**; it tells how she answered)*

a <u>public</u> company *(adj., modifies the noun company)*

a <u>publicly</u> held company *(adv., modifies the adjective **held**)*

The reporter was <u>uncertain.</u> *(adj., modifies **reporter**)*

The reporter answered <u>uncertainly.</u> *(adv., modifies **answered**)*

I feel <u>bad</u> about the mix-up. *(adj., modifies the pronoun I)*

I feel <u>badly</u> treated. *(adv., modifies the verb **treated**)*

Put modifiers where they will produce the desired meaning.

Wrong: Children are sometimes placed in Juvenile Hall because there are inadequate foster homes to meet their needs.

Right: Children are sometimes placed in Juvenile Hall because of an inadequate supply of foster homes.

Wrong: This page was left intentionally blank.

Right: This page was intentionally left blank.

Have you chosen the best modifier for the job?

> **Wrong:** The chemical dissolves readily and only a small dose can be fatal.

A large dose cannot? Replacing *only* with *even* makes it a sensible sentence.

In general, place modifiers close to the words they modify. **Misplaced modifiers** are often ambiguous or unintentionally funny.

> The patient has had chest pain when she lies on her left side for over a year.

> The chimpanzees were observed using binoculars.

> Staff members should submit a completed travel voucher with the required receipts attached to their department heads.

Dangling modifiers are another common error of placement. A dangler usually begins the sentence; what it modifies has been omitted.

> Checking the records, the error was found.

Since "the error" cannot have been "checking the records," the opening phrase is left dangling. Add the correct subject to the main clause to remedy the situation.

> Checking the records, Analisa found the error.

Here are some other dangling modifiers. Watch for such illogical constructions and rewrite to include the correct subject.

> **Dangler:** Walking along the tracks, the train whistled in the distance.
> **Correct:** Walking along the tracks, I heard the train whistle in the distance.

> **Dangler:** Having read the instructions carefully, my bicycle was easily assembled.
> **Correct:** Having read the instructions carefully, I was able to assemble my bicycle easily.

> **Dangler:** On arriving at the third floor, her apartment is the first door on the left.
> **Correct:** On arriving at the third floor, you will find her apartment is the first door on the left.

Not all dangling modifiers are as easy to detect as they are in the above examples. I found a more subtle dangler in the following sentence from a letter to shareholders. As written, the person writing the letter will be the one receiving the monthly dividends! The sentence breaks several other good-writing rules as well: It's pompous, wordy, too long, and uses the passive voice.

> In addition to receiving a monthly dividend, we believe this transaction to be beneficial to you because it allows you to participate more directly in the ongoing opportunities presented by deregulation and consolidation in the utility industry.

Here's my slimmed-down and corrected version:

> Your investment will not only continue to pay monthly dividends but will be part of the business opportunities that follow as regulations change and companies merge in the utility industry.

Verbs
Use the correct verb tense.
The correct tense comes naturally to most native-born writers. A tense that sounds right probably is right.

Present:	I walk
Past:	I walked
Future:	I will walk
Present Perfect:	I have walked (an action that began in the past and continues or is completed in the present)
Past Perfect:	I had walked (an action that began and was completed in the past)

Future Perfect:	I will have walked (an action that will begin in the future and be completed by a specific time)

Yesterday I was a dog. Today I'm a dog. Tomorrow I'll probably still be a dog. Sigh. There's so little hope for advancement.—*Snoopy (Charles Schulz)*

Where problems usually arise is in maintaining logical consistency. If you have chosen the present tense to describe a marketing study ("Our survey shows..."), use the present tense throughout ("that both men and women prefer..."). Especially when editing a long document, read it once just to check whether you have used tenses logically and consistently.

Here are two examples where decisions about verb tense are needed.

He <u>wondered</u> whether the system (is) (was) fair.
    past tense

Next, the manager <u>explains</u> how the system (works)
             present tense
(worked).

In these examples, the tense of the first verbs (*wondered, explains*) dictates the tense of verbs that follow. Thus, *was* and *works* are the correct choices.

An exception is a statement of "universal truth" which calls for the present tense even when the main verb is in the past tense.

> Newton <u>discovered</u> that apples <u>fall.</u>
>   past tense   present tense

> Benjamin Franklin <u>knew</u> that creditors <u>have</u> better
>   past tense   present tense
> memories than debtors.

The first verb in each of the following examples is in the perfect tense. What is the correct tense for subsequent verbs? (The choices are shown in parentheses.)

> They would have liked (to be) (to have been) the winners.
> Johnson has enjoyed (being) (having been) governor.
> It would have been easy for the department (to change) (to have changed) the procedure.

Piling up perfect tenses has an almost tongue-twisting effect (e.g., *would have liked to have been*). Logic suggests that you should keep subsequent verbs in the present tense, unless their action precedes the main verb. Correct choices in these examples are as follows:

> They would have liked to be the winners.
> Johnson has enjoyed being governor.
> It would have been easy for the department to change the procedure.

Use the correct mood.

Most of our sentences are in the indicative mood.

> Invention is the mother of necessity.—*Thorstein Veblen*

The interrogative mood asks a question.

> I am responsible for my actions, but who is responsible for General Motors?—*Ralph Nader*

Commands and most instructions are in the imperative mood.

> Press the red lever.

The following examples illustrate the few uses of the subjunctive mood in today's writing:

- An improbable condition or one that is contrary to fact

  If I <u>were</u> younger, I would challenge you to a match.

- An indirect command

  She specified that the money <u>be</u> donated to charity.
  His friend insisted that he <u>drive</u> the car.

- Motions and resolutions

  I move that the motion <u>be</u> adopted.
  Resolved, That the question <u>be submitted</u> to the full membership.

Shall or Will? The traditional distinction between *shall* and *will* has all but disappeared. *Will* has generally replaced *shall* in all future tenses. *Shall* still appears in some government and legal writing, where it probably results from the mistaken belief that *shall* sounds more authoritative.

> **Stilted:** The contractor shall provide all the necessary materials.

> **Natural:** The contractor will provide all the necessary materials.

Parallel Structure

Make related parts of a sentence or heading parallel in form.

This helps readers grasp the connection between the parallel elements and thus helps them understand your meaning. Aesthetics and dramatic effect are also enhanced. "Give me liberty or kill me" wouldn't have gone far in stirring patriotism.

To create parallel structure, make an infinitive parallel with an infinitive, an adjective with an adjective, and so on. In the following example, a series of active verbs is followed, unnecessarily, by a passive verb.

> Unparallel: At the meeting we will (1) discuss the proposed ordinance, (2) listen to citizen comments, (3) take a vote, and (4) the meeting will then be adjourned.
>
> Parallel: At the meeting we will (1) discuss the proposed ordinance, (2) listen to citizen comments, (3) take a vote, and (4) adjourn.

> Unparallel: A moment not only of suspense but excitement...
>
> Parallel: A moment not only of suspense but of excitement...

> Unparallel: The description was both accurate and it was easy to read.
>
> Parallel: The description was both accurate and readable.

No-Fault Sentences

Grammarians love fancy terms. Case in point: **sentence faults.** These in turn are identified as **fragments** and **run-ons.** A run-on is further described as a **fused sentence** and a **comma**

splice. Though a fragment is occasionally useful, a run-on is always against the rules. Let's go into the whys and wherefores.

Use fragments with care.

A *fragment* is a partial sentence; it may lack a subject or predicate, and it does not express a complete thought. The *Dictionary of Modern English Usage* calls fragments "verbless sentences" that enliven writing by making it more like spoken language. Fragments are appropriate in dialogue or in a question-and-answer format.

Will they win? Not if we can help it.

Use fragments sparingly for emphasis or to achieve a particular effect.

Our guarantee is good for one year. Without exception.

Avoid fragments in formal writing. If you have trouble detecting fragments, study the following examples.

Fragment: Knowing that the meeting would be disrupted if she arrived late.
Complete: Knowing that the meeting would be disrupted if she arrived late, she was careful to be on time.

Fragment: Long but incomplete thoughts that masquerade, right up to the end, as complete thoughts.
Complete: Watch out for long but incomplete thoughts that masquerade, right up to the end, as complete thoughts.

Fragment: When I think I know all the answers.
Complete: When I think I know all the answers, life asks some more questions.

Avoid run-ons.

Run-ons are two independent clauses joined only by a comma (a *comma splice*) or by no punctuation (a *fused sentence*). If the clauses are closely related, rewrite run-ons by joining the clauses with a semicolon. But if you want a stronger break, separate a run-on into two sentences.

> **Run-on:** I had another flying lesson today I learned how to stall the plane.

> **Correct:** I had another flying lesson today; I learned how to stall the plane.

Run-ons with the word *however* are especially common.

> **Run-on:** We had planned to move into the new building in May, however, construction delays forced us to change our plans.

> **Correct:** We had planned to move into the new building in May. However, construction delays...

8 Second-Level Editing: Mechanical Style

> Each communication is a challenge to the writer to present information and ideas directly and forcefully, to help the reader along, and to affect the reader in a chosen way.—*Robert Barrass*

When you edit for mechanical style, you check such matters as spelling, capitalization, abbreviations, and word division. You also review numbers (should they be words or figures?) and document appearance and integrity (are tables missing? are there gaps in page numbers?). These elements of style distinguish a polished document from a flawed one.

A style sheet will help you keep track of the choices you have made: capitalization (Co-Prosperity Spheres), hyphenation (non-aligned nations), number treatment (three million or 3 million), spellings (catalog or catalogue). The rules and tables in this section will help you put the finishing touches on your writing; a style sheet will make sure that you've been consistent. (How to make a style sheet is covered on p. 23).

Abbreviations

Abbreviations are seldom appropriate in formal business writing or general writing such as fiction, history, or news. They suggest that you have sloppy writing habits or were too hurried to complete the words. But some words are always abbreviated (for example, *Mr.*), and certain abbreviations are acceptable if space is tight or they avoid cumbersome repetition.

Abbreviations are acceptable in footnotes, tables, lists, and bibliographies. Technical writing also makes heavy use of them. (Technical writers should refer to a style guide for their particular discipline for the final word on abbreviations.) The following paragraphs present rules for abbreviation in business writing and in writing for publication.

In general, give the full name or term the first time it appears, followed by the abbreviated version in parentheses. Then use only the abbreviation throughout the remainder of the document.

The trend is away from the use of periods, especially with units of measurement (lb, km) and with abbreviations consisting entirely of capital letters (IRS, FDR). However, periods can be used if needed to prevent confusion when the abbreviated form spells a word (in., No.). Do not use periods with acronyms (NASA, URL) or with shortened forms of words (typo, stereo, the Fed, co-op, fax, caps).

To make an abbreviation or acronym plural, add a lowercase *s*.

    IQs
    MVPs

If the abbreviation has periods, add 's.

    Ph.D.'s

Do not begin a sentence with a symbol or abbreviation other than a social title (Ms., Dr., Mrs.).

Correct: Dr. Singh will be retiring in May.

Wrong: No. 5 shaft was the scene of the cave-in.
Correct: Number 5 shaft was the scene of the cave-in.
Better: The cave-in occurred in the No. 5 shaft.

Names and Titles

Ms.	Messrs.	Sr.	Ph.D.	M.P.
Mrs.	Mmes.	Esq.	M.A.	D.V.M.
Mr.	Jr.	M.D.	J.D.	

Note: Abbreviations are acceptable in captions (e.g., Dist. Atty. Shirley Ramos, Sen. Phil Bingham).

WRONG:	RIGHT:
Hon. Sawyer	the Honorable Deborah Sawyer, Hon. Deborah Sawyer
Rev. Angell	the Reverend Henry Angell, Rev. Henry Angell
Gen. Brook	General Brook, Gen. Donald E. Brook
Sen. Bingham	Senator Bingham, Senator Phil Bingham
D.A. Ramos	District Attorney Shirley Ramos
Dr. Samuel Stevens, M.D.	Samuel Stevens, M.D.
Mr. Owen Mills, Esq.	Owen Mills, Esq.
Professor Janice Young, Ph.D.	Janice Young, Ph.D. *or* Professor Janice Young

Agencies and Organizations

AAAS	ILGWU
AFL-CIO	IOOF
CAB	NFL
CBS	SAE
FDA	SBA

Write out company names without abbreviations in straight text (Union Pacific Railway), unless the company is known primarily by its abbreviated form (IBM).

The words *Inc.* and *Ltd.* are usually dropped. Use a firm's letterhead as a guide to the preferred abbreviated form for such terms as Brothers (Bros.), Company (Co.), and (&), Corporation (Corp.), and Incorporated (Inc.).

If space is limited, abbreviate the following in addresses:

Agency (Agcy.)
Department (Dept.)
Division (Div.)
Headquarters (Hdqrs. or HQ)
Institute (Inst.)
Subsidiary (Subs.)

Geographical Terms

N E S W   NE SE SW NW   ENE SSW NNE
E by SE   N by NW

St. Louis, St. Paul, *but* Fort Worth, Port Arthur, Mount Vernon

UK, UAR *or* U.K., U.A.R.

U.S. Department of Agriculture, U.S.S. Enterprise, U.S. Circuit Court

Abbreviate *United States* only when it is an adjective.

> He was glad to return to the United States.

> They felt that <u>U.S.</u> foreign policy was misguided.
> adjective

Use two capital letters *with no period* to abbreviate states in mailing addresses: AL, CO, MA (*not* AL., CO.). You may use traditional state abbreviations (Colo., Mass.) in captions or footnotes, but do not abbreviate state names in text.

Dates and Times

> Jan., Feb., Mar., Apr., May, June, July, Aug., Sept., Oct., Nov., Dec.
> **or** Ja, F, Mr, Ap, My, Je, Jl, Au, S, O, N, D
> Mon., Tues., Wed., Thurs., Fri., Sat., Sun.
> sec   min   hr (or h)   da (or d)   wk   mo   yr
> a.m. **or** A.M. (*ante meridiem*)
> p.m. **or** P.M. (*post meridiem*)
> M. (noon, *meridies*)

Parts of Books or Documents

Abbreviate references to parts of books or documents only when they appear in parentheses: (Chap. 4) or (Par. 9a).

Constitutions and Bylaws

Spell out *Section* and *Article* the first time; abbreviate them thereafter.

> SECTION 1, ARTICLE 1
> SEC. 2, ART. 2

If you are uncertain about the correct abbreviation of a term, consult a good dictionary.

Capitalization

Capital letters make a word stand out. The words we capitalize reveal what we think is important or deserves emphasis. However, not everyone agrees on what is important. I have drawn on modern authorities for the following guidelines, but I've tempered them with a few prejudices of my own.

An example is the word *federal*. Some manuals specify lowercase, unless the word is part of a proper name (Federal Trade Commission). Others capitalize *federal* everywhere (Federal government, Federal agencies). I prefer lowercase, but as long as you are consistent, you have considerable latitude in such gray areas.

First Words

Capitalize the first word of a sentence.

> A hospital should also have a recovery room adjoining the cashier's office.—*Francis O'Walsh*

> Should the employees be notified? Which ones? How?

Capitalize the first word of a quotation.

> "Life is what happens when you are busy making other plans." (John Lennon)

> "The cost of living has gone up," according to W. C. Fields, "another dollar a quart."

Notice the lowercase *a* in the word "another" in the example above; the first quoted word following an interruption is capitalized only if it begins a new sentence.

Either caps or lowercase are acceptable in numbered or outlined material, but whichever you choose, be consistent.

> Can the committee decide (a) when to meet again? (b) what topics to address?

1. Parts of Speech	*or*	1. Parts of Speech
a. noun		a. Noun
b. verb		b. Verb
c. adjective		c. Adjective

Capitalize the first word following a colon only if it begins a complete sentence.

> There are two things to aim at in life: First, get what you want; after that, enjoy it.—*Logan Pearsall Smith*

> There are three kinds of people: those who can count and those who can't.

Capitalize the first word of a resolution.

> Resolved, That proliferation of nuclear weapons be halted...

Titles, Headings, and Legends
Capitalize the first letter of the following:

* First and last words

  Pride and Prejudice

- All important words (nouns, pronouns, adjectives, adverbs, verbs, and subordinate conjunctions such as *although, because, since, unless, whether*)

  "I'll Be Seeing You"
  Conditions Following Hurricane Hilda
  Life Down Under: A Visit to Australia
  Legal Aspects of Your Software

- The first word of a hyphenated compound

  Defense Spending Re-examined

- The second word of a hyphenated compound if it's a noun or has the same force as the first word

  Cross-Country Skiing

Do **not** capitalize the first letter of the following:

- Articles (*a, an, the*), unless they are the first word or follow a dash or colon

  How a First Book Became a Best-Seller
  In Search of Funding: A Quick Guide

- Prepositions, unless they are the first or last word or are an inseparable part of a verb

  Wind in the Willows
  For Whom the Bell Tolls
  "Fixing Up a Brownstone"

- The *to* in infinitives

  How to Write a Readable Business Report

- The second word of a hyphenated compound when it modifies the first word or when the words are considered a unit

    The Co-pilot's Handbook
    Free-for-alls in the Nation's Capital

Parts of a Book

Style guides vary in their treatment of parts of a book or literary work: chapter 2 or Chapter 2. I prefer the capitalized version, because Chapter 2 seems like a proper noun (a specific chapter), and proper nouns are capped.

Passing reference to a table of contents, glossary, bibliography, and index appears in lowercase:

    In his introduction, Huxley states...

but cross-references require capitals:

    Additional sources are listed in the Bibliography.

Names and Terms

Capitalize proper names or nouns (names of specific people or places).

    Alexis de Tocqueville
    Alexander the Great
    American Telephone & Telegraph Company
    the Astrodome
    Atlanta Braves
    the Big Apple
    the Biltmore Hotel
    First Lady Martha Washington (the First Lady)

the Los Angeles Music Center
Washington, D.C.
Wild Bill Hickok
William Carlos Williams

Use lowercase for most words derived from proper nouns: arabic numerals, french fries, swiss cheese, venetian blinds, diesel engine, roman numerals, vulcanize, watt, klieg lights.

Capitalize personal titles (professional, religious, military, and civil) that immediately precede a person's name.

President Washington
Chief Justice Peter Mendosa
General Manager Sellars
Admiral Lesley Chang
Rabbi Weiss
The Reverend Audrey McIntosh

Use lowercase when such titles are part of an appositive.

Reade A. Seymour, superintendent of schools,
Susan Ferraro, chief horticulturist,
Andrew Washington, professor of astronomy,
Malcolm R. Keynes, president of the United States,
the president of XYZ Corporation, Robert S. Barron,
Canadian prime minister, Bernadette Bayer,
the governor of Nebraska, Frank Meyers,

Also note the following usage:

the President, the Vice President (when referring to the incumbent U.S. official)
the presidential yacht

the dean's office, the Dean's List

Rhodes scholar

Pardon me, Governor, will you make a statement?

The president of Techniplex will visit the company's Texas
plant next week.

Geopolitical Terms

Capitalize words such as *state*, *avenue*, *city*, or *valley* when they
follow and are part of a specific name. Use lowercase when
they precede the name or stand alone.

the Australian Outback, the Outback

the East, West, North, South (U.S.)

eastern time zone, southern accent, west of town, south of
the border

the equator, the Equatorial Current

the Gulf Stream

Long Island, a Caribbean island

New York City, the city of New York

Palos Verdes Peninsula (the proper name of a town), *but* the
San Francisco peninsula (a general description)

the Province of Quebec, the province

the Republican party, the Democrats, the Labor government

Southern Hemisphere

southern Texas, upstate New York

the Stone Age, the Jurassic period

Tenth Congressional District

the Versailles Treaty, the treaty of Versailles

Washington State, the state of Washington

the White House

Lowercase a plural generic term when it follows more than one name.

>the John Hancock and Empire State buildings
>the Missouri and Ohio rivers

Capitalize generic terms that precede more than one name.

>Mounts McKinley and Rainier
>Lakes Onandaga and Cayuga

Organizations, Institutions, Companies

>Center for Defense Information
>Girl Scouts
>Humane Society
>Periwinkle Press
>Scripps Institution
>Society for the Preservation of Barber-Shop Quartets
>Stanford University

Calendar

Capitalize days of the week, months, and holidays (President's Day, Fourth of July). For A.M. and P.M., use small caps, if available; otherwise use lowercase: a.m., p.m.

Lowercase seasons (spring, fall) and time zones (central daylight time, Pacific standard time).

Religious Terms

>Allah, Buddha, Elohim, Holy Father, Jesus Christ, the Messiah, Mohammed, the Supreme Being, Mater Dolorosa, Ayotollah

Old Testament, the Koran, King James Version, Dead Sea Scrolls

Gnosticism, Sufi, Baha'i Faith, Presbyterian, Seventh-day Adventist

Ark of the Covenant, Garden of Eden, Ecce Homo, the Diaspora, the Crusades, the Hegira, the Inquisition

Scientific Terms

Genus is capitalized, species lowercased; both are set in italic type.

Homo sapiens

Larger divisions (phylum, class, order, family) are capitalized and set in roman type.

Chordata
Primates

English words derived from the scientific terms are lowercased.

primates
omnivores

Only proper names that are part of a medical term or physical law are capitalized.

Rhys' syndrome
Faraday's constant
Hodgkin's disease

The names of chemical elements and compounds are lower-cased when written out and capitalized when appearing as chemical symbols.

    sodium chloride   NaCl

Trademarks

The *Chicago Manual of Style* says a "reasonable effort" should be made to capitalize products that are protected by trademarks: Seven-Up, Tylenol, Teflon, Kleenex, Xerox. Unless you have a reason for promoting a trademarked product, use generic terms: adhesive bandage, instead of Band-Aid; photocopy, instead of Xerox. On the other hand, whoever heard of an adhesive-bandage solution?

Military Terms

    82nd Airborne Division
    98th Field Artillery
    the Allies, the Union soldiers, the Rebels, the Red Coats
        Army headquarters
    Napoleonic Wars
    Purple Heart
    Sergeant William Posner, the sergeant
    Seventh Fleet, the fleet
    United States Navy, the navy, the U.S. Navy, the U.S.S.
        New Jersey, Arkansas National Guard, the guard
    Victoria Cross
    War of 1812

Computer Terminology

Writers in the field of computers are developing their own rules of style. Acronyms abound (SCSI, BIOS). Computer functions are given initial caps (Enter; Find and Replace), while computer languages appear either with initial caps (Java) or all caps (COBOL). Compounds are treated as one word (laptop, backup), hyphenated (hand-held), and two words (screen saver). Caps pop up in the middle of some compounds (ScanDisk, FlameThrower); hyphens are found in e-commerce, but not in eFilter.

To some extent, you can write your own rules. The overriding considerations are consistency and ease of understanding. Keep track of the choices you make on a style sheet (see p. 24).

Numbers

The following rules will help you decide whether to express numbers as figures (1, 2, 3) or words (one, two, three).

In business or technical writing or in journalism, use words for numbers 1 through 9; use figures for 10 or above.

> There were three applicants for the job.
> There were 12 applicants for the job.

In writing with a literary flavor, the dividing point is 100 instead of 10.

If a sentence or paragraph has related numbers that are both above and below 10, write the related numbers as figures.

> The three lines had 9, 12, and 15 applicants.
> (**Three** is not related to the other numbers and thus follows the previous rule.)

Spell out numbers that begin a sentence; if a related number appears in the same sentence, write it as a word, too.

> Fifty million Frenchmen can't be wrong.

> Twenty members voted yes; fifteen voted no. (*Not* Twenty members voted yes; 15 voted no.)

> One dollar out of every ten earned goes into health care.

Express large numbers in figures or in mixed figure-word form, but be consistent.

> $10,000,000 or $10 million
> 5.7 billion
> 3-¹/₂ million

Use figures for dates, as follows:

> July 4, 1776 *or* 4 July 1776
> 7/4/76 *or* 7/4/1776 (U.S.)
> 4/7/76 *or* 4/7/1776 (U.K.)

Because of the confusion that might result from the numbered form, writing the month as a word is preferred.

Use figures with units of time or measurement.

> 10 a.m., 9 o'clock
> 32 degrees Fahrenheit
> 2 half-gallons
> $^1/_2$-inch pipe
> 20 kilometers
> 3-$^1/_2$ yards
> 3-foot ruler
> 1 x 8 inches
> 8-$^1/_2$ by 11 inch paper
> 55 MPH
> 35-mm camera
> a 40-hour week, *but* forty 50-cent stamps

Use figures in the following cases:

> a vote of 5 to 4
> a score of 14-0
> a 3-for-1 stock split
> divide by 2
> an increase of 4.65
> 50 cents
> a population of 10,372
> Suite 1152

Use words in the following cases:

> thousands of refugees
> losses in the millions
> twelve hundred words

a population of about fifty thousand
one-half of the work force
in their sixties *or* in their 60s

Commas

Americans and British use commas to separate long numbers into groups of three digits (10,576,435). The European practice calls for spaces or periods (4 000 000 or 4.000.000).

Companies often have a style manual that dictates whether to use commas in a four-digit number that appears in the text (3,500 or 3500). In all cases, alignment of tabular matter requires commas when there are four or more digits.

```
 3,500
17,100
   619
 6,800
```

Commas are not used in the following:

- Page numbers (p. 1142)

- Serial numbers (73027894WG)

- Radio frequency (1330 kilocycles)

- To the right of the decimal point (1.53858)

Spelling

Misspelled words in business letters or manuscripts present your message in a flawed way. They also increase the likelihood of your being misunderstood and suggest that you are too lazy to use a dictionary.

Becoming a good speller is largely a matter of attitude. Once you are convinced that correct spelling is important, you will find the moments needed to look up and memorize difficult words. Make a list of the words that give you the most trouble, and update it as you master each one.

If a dictionary lists a second spelling, separated from the main entry by a comma or the word *or*, both spellings are considered acceptable (*ax, axe*). If the second spelling is separated by a period and introduced by the word *Also*, the main entry is preferred (*esophagus.... Also oesophagus*).

The following guidelines focus on some of the most common spelling problems.

Suffixes

-ance or -ence. When the final *c* or *g* has a soft sound, use *-ence*, *-ent*, or *-ency*.

> obsolescence, magnificent, emergency, indigent

When the final *c* or *g* has a hard sound, use *-ance*, *-ant*, or *-ancy*.

> significant, extravagance

-able or -ible. Words that have an *-ation* form usually take *-able*.

> dispensable (dispensation)
> irritable (irritation)
> quotable (quotation)
> imaginable (imagination)

Words that have an *-ive*, *-tion*, *-sion*, or *-id* form usually take *-ible*.

> combustible (combustion)
> reversible (reversion)
> collectible (collective)
> digestible (digestion)

Exceptions: definable (definition), sensible (sensation)

-ceed, -cede, or -sede. Three words end with *-ceed* and one with *-sede*.

> exceed
> proceed
> succeed
> supersede

All others ending in this syllable are spelled *-cede*: accede, concede, precede, secede, etc.

-ize or -ise. In general, this verb suffix is spelled *-ize* in the United States (ostracize, sterilize) and *-ise* in the U.K. (ostracise, sterilise). However, the preferred spelling in the U.S. of the following words is *-ise*.

> advertise
> chastise
> exorcise
> franchise

Adding Suffixes
When a word ends in a silent *e*, drop the *e* if the suffix begins with a vowel.

> dance, dancing
> make, making
> smile, smiling
> use, usable

Exceptions: mileage, shoeing, and words ending in a soft *c* or *g* (enforceable, manageable).

Retain the silent *e* if the suffix begins with a consonant.

> grate, grateful
> late, lately

Exceptions: abridgment, acknowledgment, awful, judgment, wholly, wisdom, and such words as duly and argument, in which the silent *e* is immediately preceded by a vowel other than *e*.

When a word ends in *ie*, change the *i* to *y* and drop the *e*.

die, dying
lie, lying

When a word ending in *y* is preceded by a vowel, retain the *y*.

buy, buyer
destroy, destroyer
enjoy, enjoyment

Exceptions: daily, gaiety, laid, paid, said

If the *y* is preceded by a consonant, change the *y* to *i*.

body, bodily
dry, drier (i.e., more dry)
happy, happiness
hazy, hazier

Exceptions: fryer, dryer (an appliance), and others formed from one-syllable words such as shy and wry; also, the words baby, lady, and the suffixes -ship (ladyship) and -like (city-like).

When a root word ends with a consonant that is preceded by a single vowel and the suffix begins with a vowel, double the consonant.

control, controlled
forget, forgetting
occur, occurrence
program, programmer
refer, referred
regret, regrettable

remit, remittance
transfer, transferring

Exceptions: buses, busing, transferable, and words where the accent moves from the last syllable to a preceding one (prefer, preference).

Do not double the final consonant in the following cases:

- If the suffix begins with a consonant

  commit, commitment

- If the final consonant is preceded by more than one vowel

  congeal, congealed

- If the word is accented on any syllable except the last

  bias, biased

Exceptions: handicapped, monogrammed, outfitter.

When the word ends in *c*, add a *k* in order to retain the hard sound.

mimicking
picnicking
politicking
shellacked

Plurals

Most nouns are made plural by adding s.

alibis	paths
beliefs	plaintiffs
locks	values

But if the word ends in *s*, *x*, *ch*, *sh*, *z* or *j*, add *es*.

   trenches
   bushes
   dresses
   boxes
   waltzes

If a noun ending in *y* is preceded by a consonant, change the *y* to *i* and add *es*.

   cities
   levies
   countries
   stories
   families

Note: Proper names ending in *y* usually retain the *y* in their plural form.

   two hot Julys
   the Ogilvys

Exceptions: the Rockies, the Alleghenies

Some nouns that end in *f*, *ff*, or *fe* are made plural by changing the *f* to *v* and adding *es*.

   knives
   shelves
   halves
   lives

Some of these have two forms.

    scarves, scarfs
    loaves, loafs
    wharves, wharfs

Some nouns ending in *f* do not change when made plural.

    chefs
    chiefs

If a noun ending in *o* is preceded by a vowel, add *s*.

    cameos
    ratios
    studios
    zoos

If the *o* is preceded by a consonant, an *es* is often added.

    tomatoes
    echoes
    torpedoes
    heroes

Some of the more than 40 exceptions to this rule are silos, commandos, mementos, and musical terms such as solos, banjos, and pianos.

Some nouns have the same form for singular and plural.

    sheep
    deer
    corps
    scissors
    remains
    offspring

Some nouns change internally to indicate the plural form.

tooth, teeth
mouse, mice
woman, women

Hard-to-Spell Words

Many difficult words simply have to be memorized, but this is not hard to do. You soon develop a sense of whether a word "looks right." When in doubt, look it up.

The following words frequently show up on lists of spelling bugaboos.

accommodate
accumulate
acknowledgment
all right
consensus
embarrass
existence
harass
inoculate
irrelevant
judgment
liaison
lightning
maintenance
maneuver
miscellaneous
parallel
prerogative

pseudonym
recommend
renaissance
rhythm
surprise
weird

Quotations

Capitalize the first word in a quotation, unless an ellipsis (...) indicates that the quotation begins in mid-sentence.

> "It's bad to suppress laughter," Fred Allen once said, adding that "it goes right back down and spreads to your hips."

In legal or scholarly writing, use brackets to show where you have added a word or capital letter.

> The history of our time is a history of phrases, which rise to great power and then suddenly pass away: "the merchants of death,"... "America first," "cash and carry,"... "bring the boys home,"... [F]ew men have had either the courage or the resources to stand up to these shibboleths.—*Russell Davenport*

With quotations of more than one paragraph, you have two choices.

- Place quotation marks at the beginning of each paragraph but at the end of only the final paragraph.

- Indent the quotation as a block and use no quotation marks.

Do not use quotation marks in the following cases:

> Charles Dudley Warner observed that the thing generally raised on city land is taxes.

> The question remained, Who was responsible?

> Samuel Clemens, better known as Mark Twain...

> The so-called gender gap has taken on political overtones. (not the so-called "gender gap")

> Learning when to say No is an important lesson in business.

Word Division

A word processor does a good job of dividing words at the right-hand margin, so I've included only a few rules.

Word Division Do's

Divide between syllables, according to pronunciation.

> market-able, *not* mar-ketable
> dis-tant, *not* dist-ant

Divide between two consonants that are surrounded by vowels.

> mas-ter
> phar-macy
> sur-vey
> sus-tain

Divide at prefixes or suffixes that contain three or more letters.

> pre-ven-tion
> super-market

infra-red
contra-band
mother-hood
pseudo-science

Divide between doubled consonants unless they are at the end of the root word.

com-mit-tee
book-keeper
but-ter
can-non
recur-ring
swim-ming
run-ning
plan-ning
forestall-ing

Word Division Don'ts
Don't divide one-syllable words.

thought
screamed
lounge
noise
burned
dumped

Don't divide one-letter syllables.

omen, *not* o-men
alive, *not* a-live
folio, *not* foli-o

Don't divide in such a way that you create a misleading pronunciation.

> dancing, *not* danc-ing
> pred-ator, *not* pre-dator
> subtle, *not* sub-tle
> hoping, *not* hop-ing

Don't carry a two-letter syllable over to the next line.

> leader, *not* lead-er
> fainted, *not* faint-ed

Don't separate abbreviations and figures.

> 200 B.C., *not* 200/B.C.
> 1:00 a.m., *not* 1:00/a.m.
> 150 km, *not* 150/km

Try to avoid dividing personal names, but if necessary, break after the middle initial.

> Julia E./Pascuale
> M. V./Thomas

Don't separate the elements of an outline or list, such as (a) or (1), from what follows them; carry such marks over to the next line.

> **Wrong:** The program to redevelop the inner city will include (a) an environmental impact report, (b) sources of funding...

> **Right:** The program to redevelop the inner city will include (a) an environmental impact report, (b) sources of...

Don't divide the last word of more than two consecutive lines.

Don't divide the last word of a paragraph or the last word on a right-hand page.

Document Integrity

Seemingly trivial errors in assembling a document distract the reader's attention from your ideas. A document may be 99 percent error-free, but the 1 percent with errors is what's noticed.

The changes made during editing increase the chance of a mismatch between parts of a document. Gaps in numbering, missing figures or tables, and discrepancies between the table of contents and text are typical slipups. Edit for this kind of integrity with a separate pass through a document, checking the following elements.

Numbering

Are pages, sections, and chapters numbered sequentially? Are cross-references correct? Are references to other documents numbered sequentially and listed in that order in a bibliography?

Figures and Tables

Are figures and tables numbered sequentially? Is the numbering style consistent (e.g., arabic or roman numerals, hyphenation, decimals)? Is the format and style of captions uniform? Are the titles or captions of any figures or tables identical? If so, change one of them so that readers can distinguish between them. Did you misplace a modifier in a caption?

> Shirley Hansen greets her family after three years in O'Hare Airport.

Table of Contents
Does the text for all of the headings cited in the table of contents still exist? Are the headings correctly worded? Are the page numbers correct?

Page Layouts
Do running heads (chapter or section titles that appear at the top of each page) match the text? Are numbered footnotes sequential?

Parallelism
Is every subparagraph (a) followed by subparagraph (b)? Is (i) followed by (ii)?

Document Appearance
A reader's first impression of what you have written is visual. Keep the goal of a pleasing presentation in mind as you make decisions about the appearance of a document.

Spacing is key. Information is more readily absorbed if it isn't too densely packed, so create plenty of white space around your words.

Indented portions of text and bulleted information are eye-catching, and an outline format is occasionally useful to emphasize the organization of your material.

Should you add chapter headings? Section headings or footings? They can help the reader find a specific part of a long document. Location of page numbers is another variable; try several locations and decide.

Are the page breaks satisfactory? Printers advise you to avoid the following "bad breaks."

- Short line at the top of a page (called a *widow*)

- Heading at the bottom of a page (at least two lines of text should follow a heading)

- A page that ends with a hyphenated word (some accept such a break on a left-hand page)

- A quoted portion that begins on the last line or ends on the first line of a page (at least two lines of the quotation should appear in either place)

- A footnote that is not on the same page as its original citation (if the first two lines are on the same page, the footnote can be continued on the following page)

Desktop publishing software comes loaded with options: justified margins, a wide variety of fonts and sizes, italic and boldface type, multiple columns, drop caps, and so on. The type of document (or in-house policy) may determine these choices.

As you examine the final document, divorce yourself from its content and consider only its visual impact. Although you want to take advantage of the opportunities for adding graphic interest to text, keep in mind that ease of reading comes first. The reader should not have to struggle to see text that's overlaid on graphics or printed in eye-catching colors that reduce legibility. Graphic images should complement text, not compete with it.

> Nothing you write, if you hope to be good, will ever come out as you first hoped.—*Lillian Hellman*

Good writing comes from good rewriting. It's a dynamic process that presents challenges and provides satisfactions whenever you put words together. I hope you find *Rewrite Right!* a helpful guide along the way.

Glossary

Adjective. A word that describes or limits the meaning of a noun or noun phrase.

> Niagara Falls is simply a <u>vast, unnecessary</u> amount of water going the wrong way and then falling over <u>unnecessary</u> rocks.—*Oscar Wilde*

Adverb. A word that modifies or expands the meaning of a verb, adjective, or other adverb.

> ...There is no <u>distinctively</u> native American criminal class except Congress.—*Mark Twain*

Alliteration. The use of words that begin with or contain the same letter or sound, in order to achieve a certain effect.

> Finding Facts Fast
> Write Right! A Desk Drawer Digest...

Antecedent. The word, phrase, or clause referred to by a pronoun. Skilled writers avoid ambiguous antecedents. See p. 55 and p. 124.

> I'm a great believer in <u>luck</u>, and I find that the harder
> antecedent
> I work, the more I have of <u>it</u>.—*Thomas Jefferson*
> pronoun

Antonym. A word having a meaning opposite to the meaning of another word. See Synonym.

> slow/fast
> hot/cold
> difficult/easy

Appositive. A noun or phrase that identifies the preceding word or concept.

> Gabriel Garcia Marquez, the Nobel laureate,...
> my supervisor, Jack Campbell,...

Article. The words *a*, *an*, and *the*. Usually classified as adjectives.

Case. The inflection or change made to a pronoun in order to show its relation to other words. Pronouns in the **nominative** case are subjects of verbs (*we*); in the **objective** case pronouns are objects of verbs or prepositions (*us*); and in the **possessive** case pronouns show possession (*our*). See p. 121.

> <u>We</u> gave <u>them</u> <u>our</u> answer.

We is the subject of the verb *gave*, *them* is its indirect object, and *our* shows possession of the noun *answer*.

Clause. A group of words that contains a subject and predicate. An **independent** clause expresses a complete thought. A **dependent** (subordinate) clause does not express a complete thought and depends on the main (independent) clause to complete its meaning.

If you aren't fired with enthusiasm,
dependent clause
you will be fired with enthusiasm.—*Vince Lombardi*
independent clause

A **restrictive** clause is necessary to define or limit the word it modifies; it is not set off by commas.

My clothes are addressed to women
who can afford to travel with forty suitcases.
restrictive clause
—*Yves Saint Laurent*

A **nonrestrictive** clause adds information but does not limit what it modifies; it is set off by commas.

To say nothing, especially when speaking,
nonrestrictive clause
is half the art of diplomacy.—*Will and Ariel Durant*

Cliché. An expression that has become dull and unoriginal by overuse.

Clichés should be avoided like the plague.

Complement. A word or phrase that completes the meaning of the verb.

The judge named Sanchez <u>jury foreman</u>.

We found their argument <u>unconvincing</u>.

Happiness is <u>having a scratch for every itch</u>.—*Ogden Nash*

Compound. Consisting of two or more elements.

How can one conceive of a <u>one-party</u> system in a country
compound adjective
that has over two hundred varieties of cheese?
—*Charles deGaulle*

<u>The wisdom of the wise and the experience of the ages</u>
compound subject
are perpetuated by quotations.—*Benjamin Disraeli*

I <u>hate and regret</u> the failure of my marriages.
 compound verb
—*J. Paul Getty*

Compound words are classified as temporary, permanent, open, and closed. A **temporary** compound consists of words joined by the writer for a momentary purpose.

Love is <u>a many-splintered</u> thing.—*R. Buckminster Fuller*

A **permanent** compound can be found in the dictionary, indicating its acceptance in our language: half-breed. An **open** compound is written as two separate words: cash crop. Write a **closed** compound as a single word: casework, paycheck.

Conjunction. A word that connects words, phrases, and clauses. **Coordinating** conjunctions (*and, but, or, nor, for, yet,* and *so*) connect elements of equal rank.

> nuts and bolts
> Tom, Dick, or Harry

Two independent clauses are joined by a coordinating conjunction.

> Music is my mistress, and she plays second fiddle to no one.—*Duke Ellington*

Coordinating conjunctions used in pairs are called **correlatives**:

> either/or
> not only/but also
> both/and

Subordinating conjunctions (*that, when, where, while, if, because, although, since,* etc.) connect elements of unequal rank (i.e., an independent and a dependent clause).

> A man in love is incomplete <u>until</u> he has married. Then he's finished.—*Zsa Zsa Gabor*

Contraction. The use of an apostrophe to indicate omitted letters or numbers.

> can't (cannot)
> '50 (1950)

Dangling modifier. A modifier that cannot logically modify any word in a sentence. See p. 127.

Having left in a hurry, his wallet was still on the dresser.

Gerund. A verb form that ends in *-ing* and is used as a noun. See Participle.

<u>Multitasking</u> is efficient.

<u>Writing</u> is the hardest way of <u>earning</u> a <u>living</u>, with the possible exception of <u>wrestling</u> alligators.—*Olin Miller*

Infinitive. The word *to* plus the present tense of a verb.

In a hierarchy every employee tends <u>to rise</u> to his level of incompetence.—*Laurence Peter*

In a **split** infinitive, a word or phrase comes between *to* and the verb.

Split: They were asked to promptly complete the questionnaire.

Improved: They were asked to complete the questionnaire promptly.

Acceptable: We expect to more than double sales next year.

Inflection. Changes in the form of a word to show grammatical functions such as case, voice, person, mood, tense, and number. Thus, inflection of the pronoun *I* to *we* shows the change from singular to plural; inflection of *I* to *me* shows the change from nominative to objective case.

Interjection. A word or phrase that expresses strong feelings; an exclamation.

> My word!
> Ouch!
> Not on your life!
> Cool!

Metaphor. The implicit comparison of concepts by substituting one concept for another in order to suggest their similarity. "The dawn of civilization" indirectly compares dawn to the early days of civilization. "The long arm of the law" gives law a human body in order to illustrate a similarity of function. See p. 84.

> Writing, like life itself, is a voyage of discovery.—*Henry Miller*

Misplaced modifier. Incorrect placement of a modifier, which produces a misleading meaning. See p. 126.

> **Misplaced:** Over one million Americans have a heart attack every year.

> **Correct:** Every year over one million Americans have a heart attack.

Mood. The change made in a verb to show whether it makes a statement (**indicative** mood), is a command (**imperative** mood), or expresses a condition contrary to fact (**subjunctive** mood). See p. 130.

Noun. A word that names things. "Things" can be physical objects (table, pen), abstract concepts (humor, truth), actions (writing, scratching), substances (air, water), measures (centimeter, inch), places (street, factory), persons (reporter, mechanic), and so on. **Proper** nouns refer to a specific person, place, or thing (Michelangelo, Houston, World War II); they are capitalized.

Parallel construction. Using grammatically parallel forms (e.g., infinitives or nouns) to emphasize the similarity or relatedness of ideas.

> **Unparallel:** The power to tax involves the power of destruction.

> **Parallel:** The power to tax involves the power to destroy.
> —*John Marshall*

Participle. A verb form used as an adjective. See Gerund.

> an <u>inspiring</u> lecture
> a <u>worn</u> collar
> the <u>outraged</u> electorate
> a <u>frozen</u> dessert
> The <u>debugging</u> procedure took only a few minutes.

Parts of speech. The classification of words according to the function they perform in a sentence: noun, pronoun, verb, adjective, adverb, preposition, conjunction, and interjection. The definition of each part of speech appears at its alphabetical entry.

Person. The speaker is the first person (*I*, *we*), the person spoken to is the second person (*you*), and the person or thing spoken of is the third person (*he*, *she*, *they*, *it*).

Phrase. A group of words that has no subject or predicate and that functions as if it were a single word.

> Turn right <u>at the signal</u>.
> prepositional phrase

> <u>Knowing the subject thoroughly</u>, she was quick to reply.
> participial phrase

Predicate. A group of words that makes a statement or asks a question about the subject of a sentence. A **simple** predicate consists of a verb; a **complete** predicate includes verbs, modifiers, objects, and complements.

> A student <u>can win twelve letters at a university without learning how to write one</u>.—*Robert Maynard Hutchins*

Prefix. A word element that is placed in front of a root word, thereby changing or modifying the meaning.

> <u>re</u>claim
> <u>mis</u>print
> <u>macro</u>cosm
> <u>un</u>easy

Preposition. A word that shows the relationship between a noun and the object of the preposition. In the sentence "She put the check in the envelope," *in* is the preposition that shows the relationship between the noun *check* and the object of the preposition *envelope*.

> The buck stops with the guy who signs the checks.—*Rupert Murdoch*

By the way, a preposition is a fine thing to end a sentence with. ☺

Pronoun. A word that takes the place of a noun and is used in order to avoid cumbersome repetition. See p. 121. **Personal** pronouns include *I, you, he, she, it* (sing.), *we, you, they* (pl.), and their inflected forms (e.g., *me, her, them, ours*).

> The very fact that <u>we</u> make such a to-do over golden weddings indicates <u>our</u> amazement at human endurance. The celebration is more in the nature of a reward for stamina.
> —*Ilka Chase*

Relative pronouns (*who, which, that,* and compounds like *whoever*) relate one part of a sentence to a word in another part.

> A government <u>that</u> robs Peter to pay Paul can always depend on the support of Paul.—*G. B. Shaw*

Indefinite pronouns include *any, some, each, every,* and compounds with *-body* and *-one,* such as *no one, everyone, somebody,* and *nobody.*

> Experience is the name <u>everyone</u> gives to their mistakes.
> —*Oscar Wilde*

Reflexive and **intensive** pronouns include *myself, themselves,* and others formed by adding *-self* or *-selves* to a personal pronoun.

Tact is the ability to describe others as they see <u>themselves</u>.—*Abraham Lincoln*

Demonstrative pronouns include *this*, *that*, *these*, and *those*.

<u>That</u> is the wrong answer.

Interrogative pronouns include *who*, *which*, and *what*.

<u>Who</u> shall guard the guardians themselves?—*Juvenal*

Sentence. A combination of words that contains at least one subject and predicate (grammatical definition); a group of words that expresses a complete thought (popular definition). Sentence structures are classified as simple, compound, and complex.

A **simple** sentence is one independent clause consisting of a subject and predicate; the sentence may have modifying phrases but no dependent clauses.

There is no abstract art. You must always start with something.—*Pablo Picasso*

A **compound** sentence is two or more independent clauses.

Blessed are the young, for they shall inherit the national debt.—*Herbert Hoover*

A **complex** sentence is one independent and one or more dependent clauses.

When ideas fail, words come in very handy.—*Johann Goethe*

Power and violence are opposites; where one rules absolutely, the other is absent.—*Hannah Arendt*

Sentence functions are categorized as declarative, interrogative, imperative, and exclamatory. A **declarative** sentence makes an assertion.

> Success is simply a matter of luck. Ask any failure.—*Earl Wilson*

An **interrogative** sentence asks a question.

> How can they tell?—*Dorothy Parker, on hearing of Calvin Coolidge's death*

An **imperative** sentence issues a command.

> Don't trust anyone over thirty!—*Mario Savio*

An **exclamatory** sentence expresses a strong feeling.

> America is a mistake—a giant mistake!—*Sigmund Freud*

Sentence faults result from trying to crowd too much into a sentence (a **run-on**) or from failing to have enough in a sentence (a **fragment**). A run-on is two independent clauses joined only by a comma (called a **comma splice**):

> **Comma Splice:** We are temporarily out of widgets, however we expect a shipment within two weeks.

> **Correct:** We are temporarily out of widgets; however, we expect a shipment within two weeks.

or two independent clauses with no punctuation connecting them (called a **fused sentence**):

> **Fused Sentence:** We expect immediate payment otherwise we will turn your account over to a collection agency.

Correct: We expect immediate payment; otherwise, we will turn your account over to a collection agency.

A fragment is a partial sentence that either lacks a verb or fails to express a complete thought.

Wrong: Whenever I think I know all the answers.

Right: Whenever I think I know all the answers, life asks a few more questions.

Fragments are acceptable in questions and answers, for occasional emphasis ("Not likely."), in transitions ("On to the next point."), and in definitions. See p. 133.

Simile. A direct comparison using the word *like* or *as*. See p. 84.

Having a family is like having a bowling alley installed in your brain.—*Martin Mull*

Suffix. A word element added to the end of a root word.

geno<u>cide</u>
bore<u>dom</u>
fort<u>ify</u>
back<u>ward</u>

Synonym. A word similar in meaning to another word. See Antonym.

hazard/danger
invisible/unseen
handbook/manual

Tense. The form of a verb that shows distinctions in time: present, past, future, present perfect, past perfect, future perfect. See p. 128.

Verb. A word that asserts that something exists, has certain characteristics, or acts in a certain way. Verbs change form to indicate time (she will speak, he spoke), person (I speak, he speaks), or mood (Speak!). See p. 128.

Linking verbs, such as *to be*, *to appear*, *to become*, and *to seem*, serve as connections between the subject and its complement. (See Complement.)

> Pollution <u>is</u> nothing but resources we're not harvesting.
> —*R. Buckminster Fuller*

Transitive verbs require a direct object to complete their meaning.

> Big girls <u>need</u> big diamonds.—*Margaux Hemingway*

Intransitive verbs do not require an object.

> Society attacks early when the individual is helpless.
> —*B. F. Skinner*

Voice. The form of the verb used to express the relation between the subject and the action expressed by the verb. In the *passive voice*, the subject is acted upon; in the *active voice*, the subject performs the action. See p. 77.

Passive: The tie-breaker was won by Marisela.

Active: Marisela won the tie-breaker.

Index

Also from Jan Venolia

5 ³/₈ x 7 inches
144 pages

8 ¹/₂ x 11 inches
192 pages

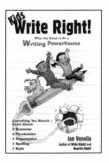

6 x 9 inches
128 pages

*Available from your local bookstore, or by ordering direct from
the publisher. Write for our catalogs of over
1,000 books and posters.*

TEN SPEED PRESS
Celestial Arts / Tricycle Press
P.O. Box 7123, Berkeley, CA 94707
www.tenspeed.com
1-800-841-2665 or fax 510-559-1629
order@tenspeed.com